D0370380

Daily Warm-Ups

ECONOMICS

Level II

The classroom teacher may reproduce materials in this book for classroom use only.

The reproduction of any part for an entire school or school system is strictly prohibited.

No part of this publication may be transmitted, stored, or recorded in any form

without written permission from the publisher.

1   2   3   4   5   6   7   8   9   10

ISBN 0-8251-6082-0

Copyright © 2006

J. Weston Walch, Publisher

P.O. Box 658 • Portland, Maine 04104-0658

www.walch.com

Printed in the United States of America

The *Daily Warm-Ups* series is a wonderful way to turn extra classroom minutes into valuable learning time. The 180 quick activities—one for each day of the school year—practice social studies skills. These daily activities may be used at the very beginning of class to get students into learning mode, near the end of class to make good educational use of that transitional time, in the middle of class to shift gears between lessons—or whenever else you have minutes that now go unused.

Daily Warm-Ups are easy-to-use reproducibles—simply photocopy the day's activity and distribute it. Or make a transparency of the activity and project it on the board. You may want to use the activities for extra-credit points or as a check on the social studies skills that are built and acquired over time.

However you choose to use them, *Daily Warm-Ups* are a convenient and useful supplement to your regular lesson plans. Make every minute of your class time count!

What Is Economics?

Economics is a social science devoted to the study of markets. Economics looks at the way society uses resources to make goods and services and then distributes these goods and services to the human population.

Think about the term *social science*. What constitutes a social science? What makes a social science different from a "hard" science, such as biology? Write your thoughts below.

1

Related Social Sciences

There are other social sciences that connect with economics. For example, economics can tell us something about factors that have driven historical events. History as a study often uses concepts from economics to explain issues such as the causes of a war, a country's population growth or decline, and an upheaval or revolution in a country's government.

Following is a list of social sciences. How are concepts from economics used for the study of each social science? Use an example from each social science to explain your answer.

    a. political science

    b. sociology

    c. history

    d. anthropology

2

Goods and Services

Economics looks at the production of goods and services and their distribution within the market. A **good** is a product that is tangible—you can hold it in your hand (an MP3 player, for example). A **service** is intangible (the transaction that took place between you and the person who sold you the MP3 player).

Think about the goods and services you use throughout your day—for example, goods that you or your family buy (such as breakfast cereal) and services that you pay for (such as paying a babysitter). Write a list of these items in the chart below. Indicate whether what is received is a good or a service. This can get tricky! Is the music you listen to on your MP3 player a good or a service? Or both?

Product received	Good	Service

Free Goods and Services

In the space below, write three goods and services that you think are free. In other words, they appear in such complete abundance that no one has to pay for them, and no one is left out. Moreover, no one has to work to produce this good or service. Can you think of three?

4

Resources

A key concept in economics is that to make the products society needs to function, we must have **resources**—all of the materials and labor that go into making products.

Think of all of the resources needed to go into making products. In the chart below, write examples of the resources given. There is a fourth resource: labor, which is the human power that goes into the production of products.

Raw materials	Information	Technology

5

What Goes into a Bicycle?

Resources include the raw materials found in nature, such as coal and oil, minerals, water, lumber, and so forth. They also include human resources in the form of labor, the development of technology, and the generation of information.

Imagine you wish to purchase a bicycle. In the space below, brainstorm all of the resources that will go into making the bicycle and selling the bicycle to you, the consumer. Make sure you add on to all of the types of resources shown in the graphic organizer. Add as many circles to the organizer as you need.

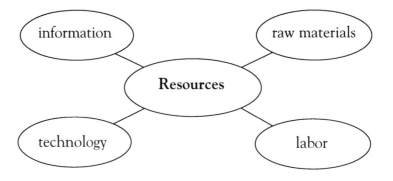

information

raw materials

Resources

technology

labor

Scarcity

One of the issues that drives the market is the fact that resources are scarce. Some resources are scarce in that they are rare, such as gold or uranium. Some are nonrenewable, such as oil. But all resources are scarce in that they require effort to make them useful to people. Even if there were an infinite supply of gold in the world, it would take time, labor, and other resources to mine gold and render it useful.

The products that people buy have their basis in a natural resource. From the list below, choose one resource that you know something about. Write a story about the resource and what happens to it to make it useful to humans. Make sure you tell whether the resource is renewable or not.

diamond	petroleum	titanium
wheat	iron	wood
cotton	coal	salt

7

Basic Economics Vocabulary

Match each economics term on the left with its definition on the
right. Write the correct letter on the line.

_____ 1. economics

_____ 2. scarcity

_____ 3. resources

_____ 4. good

_____ 5. service

a. materials and labor

b. an intangible product

c. the study of markets

d. a tangible product

e. the driving factor in consumer choice

Daily Warm-Ups: Economics

8

Consumer Choice

Economics as a study assumes that the needs of people are infinite. Therefore, the products that fulfill our needs are, logically, scarce. Scarcity leads to the concept of consumer choice. The scarcity of resources will not permit us to have everything we want all at once. We must make choices among the products available to us, both those to produce and those to buy.

One scarce, nonrenewable resource is one we don't often think about: time. It dictates how much we can accomplish in a day. What will you be doing with your time today? Write a list of what you will be doing today. Write the amount of time you will spend on each activity and what products will be generated. For example, the list you create for this activity is a product. If you are spending some time today watching television, the product could be "renewal of energy," or "relaxation," or "expansion of experience" (but only if you watch something educational!). Be creative but realistic in your description of products.

9

Cost

Time is a scarce resource. The time you spend watching television is not renewable: You cannot spend the same time doing homework. In economics, time is a feature of cost. Cost includes not only the expenditure of resources to create goods and services, but also the value placed on choosing one type of expenditure over another.

Write a list of what you will be doing today. Write the amount of time you will spend on each activity and what products will be generated. Pay yourself for each product you will generate. If you will spend some time working for pay, the salary you receive will likely pay higher than, say, watching television. Compared to watching television, how much will you pay yourself for studying?

10

What Is a Market?

A **market** is any place (from an actual building to an imagined "space") where buyers and sellers exchange resources, goods, and services. We often think of a market as being a place where end consumers buy their products and services. However, the market in a global sense includes all of the transactions that humans make, including the sale of their labor to employers and the selling of raw materials to factories.

Imagine that you are an atom of silicon. You are going to cause a number of transactions to take place before you reach your final destination inside a consumer's laptop computer. What are the market transactions that will take place for you to reach your destination? Write them below, making sure you distinguish between the buyer and the seller.

11

Market Thinking

There are many places where people come together to buy and sell. Think about what constitutes a market. In the space below, write five places, either actual places or "virtual" places, where people get together to buy and sell. Then explain what sorts of transactions take place at each. Try to include as much variety as possible in your list.

12

The Ideal Market and Economic Modeling

Economists assume certain things in order to say something about human behavior. The basis of economics is a reliance on the ideal market. Economists think about human behavior overall and then identify behaviors that are ideal. Ideal behaviors are those that are found most often and are most likely to hold true. The reality, however, is that people are unpredictable. In addition, there are a huge number of economic transactions that occur every day. The ideal market, and the economic models that are based on it, are therefore a theory based on an abstraction of human behavior.

What is a theory? How is it different from "hard" scientific fact? Explain why the ideal market is a theory and not scientific fact. How close, in your opinion, does the ideal market come to scientific fact? What scientific evidence supports the theory?

13

Ceteris Paribus

Economic modeling relies on a concept called *ceteris paribus*, a term from Latin meaning "everything else holding steady." Economists consider all the variables in the marketplace and then hold all other variables steady while they look at the effect of one variable's rise and fall. They can then discuss cause-and-effect relationships. For example, a rise in the price of soft drinks may lead to an increase in the demand for bottled water.

Consider the last test for which you received a grade. In the chart below, write three positive variables you might have had that helped you on the test. Perhaps you got a really good night's sleep or remembered to eat breakfast. Next, write three negative variables. Then determine the effect on your grade of an increase or decrease for each variable in turn, with all the other variables remaining constant.

14

Positive	Negative

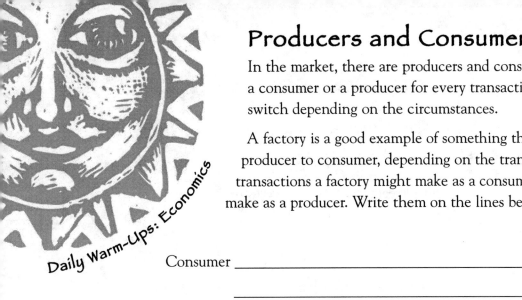

Producers and Consumers

In the market, there are producers and consumers. Not everyone is a consumer or a producer for every transaction, however. Roles switch depending on the circumstances.

A factory is a good example of something that changes roles from producer to consumer, depending on the transaction. Think of five transactions a factory might make as a consumer and three it might make as a producer. Write them on the lines below.

Consumer _____

_____

_____

_____

Producer _____

_____

_____

_____

15

Microeconomics and Macroeconomics

Economics is broken out into two categories of study, microeconomics and macroeconomics. **Microeconomics** studies how individuals in the market behave. "Individuals" in this case can refer to individual people or individual companies or firms. Microeconomics tends to aggregate the behaviors of individuals, however. This means that assumptions about what individuals do lead to determinations of how society will react as a whole to certain influences. Thus microeconomics tries to answer questions such as, "If we raise the federal minimum wage, will firms in general raise the prices of their products?"

Macroeconomics, on the other hand, looks at the behavior of the economy as a whole. This includes the U.S. market and global markets. Macroeconomics looks at issues such as the unemployment rate, the rate of inflation, and interest rates. Sometimes the two areas of study overlap. Unemployment may affect buying behavior on an individual basis, for example.

Think of issues that are often covered in the news. Describe one issue that is a concern for microeconomics and one for macroeconomics. Explain your choices.

16

Review of Economic Terms

Use the clues to fill in the crossword puzzle below.

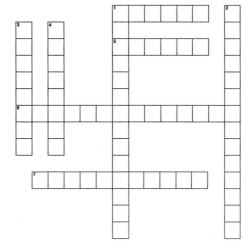

Across

1. a place where buyers and sellers exchange resources, goods, and services
5. Scarcity of resources causes consumer _____.
6. the study of individual behavior in the market
7. a market that is a theory, not a reality

Down

1. the study of the behavior of the market as a whole
2. phrase meaning "everything else held constant"
3. one who buys
4. one who creates goods or services

17

Positive and Normative

There are two ways to view economics. A **positive view** limits itself to describing economic situations and predicting what may take place in the market under different circumstances. A **normative view** looks at the market and states an opinion on how things should be.

Choose one of the following topics that tends to be in the news often. Write three sentences that describe the topic from a positive point of view and three from a normative point of view.

welfare	the minimum wage	immigration
Social Security	globalization	tax cuts for the "rich"

18

Rational Self-interest

Many theories of how the ideal market works were developed by Adam Smith (1723–1790). One theory he had was about rational self-interest. This theory states that an individual will always act in his or her own best interests. However, since everybody acts with self-interest in mind, individual acts of self-interest tend to balance others out.

Some would argue with the idea that every action we take is guided strictly by self-interest. Giving to charities, for example, is described in the economic model as a self-interested act, since giving to others makes people feel good about themselves. Do you agree with Adam Smith that every action arises from self-interest? Explain your answer.

19

Other Economic Systems

It's important to remember that capitalism is not the only economic system. Pure capitalism sits at one economic extreme. In pure capitalism, private individuals own and control property and the means of production. At the other economic extreme is pure communism, and socialism sits somewhere in the middle.

In a paragraph, describe communism and socialism. Are there any countries presently that you can think of that are purely capitalist or purely communist?

20

The "Invisible Hand"

Because factories and companies want to make money, they are guided by their own self-interest to identify what products consumers want to buy. Then they produce those products. Early economist Adam Smith called this "the invisible hand"—the market producing exactly what consumers want, thus making everyone happy.

No doubt, there have been things you wanted to buy because they filled some need or want that you had. Think about all of the products on the market today that were not available 50 years ago. Why do people need them now? Do you suppose that people 50 years ago felt that something was lacking because these products were not invented yet? How did producers determine that people would want or need these products? Describe a product that you wish someone would invent. Explain why people would want or need this product.

21

Marginal Analysis

Economists use marginal analysis to look at consumer and producer choices. For a given change to a present situation, economists ask, "How much more benefit will be gained from a change? At what point does the cost associated with a change outweigh the benefit?"

Here is an analogy for marginal analysis: Imagine that you are really hungry. You sit down to a meal and begin to eat it quickly. As you fill up, you become less hungry and more satisfied. The first bite you take has a great deal of benefit for you, the next bite slightly less benefit, the third even less, and so forth. All of the bites together add up to great benefit for you, but each bite has marginally less benefit than the one before. Eventually, you fill up completely, but you've been so hungry you do not notice. Finally, you reach a point at which the marginal cost of each bite, in terms of discomfort, outweighs the marginal benefit.

Write an analogy to describe marginal analysis.

22

More Basic Vocabulary

In the numbered column are terms important to economics. In the bottom column are definitions. Match each term with the appropriate definition. Write the correct letter on the line.

___ 1. positive

___ 2. normative

___ 3. rational self-interest

___ 4. "the invisible hand"

___ 5. marginal analysis

a. a theory that rational self-interest leads to ideal market conditions

b. a view of economics that describes and predicts

c. a way of finding the optimal level of benefit versus cost

d. the idea that individuals will always act for their own benefit

e. a view of economics that develops opinions on what should be

23

Factors of Production

Listed below are the factors of production in a market economy. Explain what each one is and its importance to the functioning of the economy. Use examples.

1. labor _____

_____

2. capital _____

_____

3. land _____

_____

4. entrepreneurship _____

_____

24

Production Vocabulary

Match each economics vocabulary term with its definition. Write the correct letter on the line.

___ 1. capital

___ 2. entrepreneur

___ 3. production possibilities

___ 4. opportunity cost

___ 5. absolute advantage

___ 6. comparative advantage

a. a person who takes on the risks of a business venture

b. the set of goods that can be produced in a given economy using all resources

c. the ability to produce a good at less opportunity cost than a trading partner

d. goods used to produce other goods

e. the ability to produce a good at less resource cost than a trading partner

f. the quantity of other goods that must be given up to obtain a good

25

Opportunity Cost

A major consideration in economics is the opportunity cost of production. Opportunity cost represents what must be given up to obtain something else. Thus, the opportunity cost for watching television might be doing homework or walking the dog. It's important to remember that determining opportunity cost does not necessarily require making value judgments. The opportunity cost for doing homework might be watching television, depending on the person's needs at the time.

Think of three activities you spent time doing yesterday. Write them below. Then, for each, write two other things that you realistically could have done instead. Explain why you chose the activities you did over the ones you could have done.

26

Production Possibilities

Imagine that a given society, called Baghina, produces only two items: hot dogs and bicycles. If everything else holds steady for all choices, what will the graph of the production possibilities look like? Using the table, draw the graph on the grid below.

Hot Dogs	Bicycles
100	0
90	4
75	8
50	12
0	16

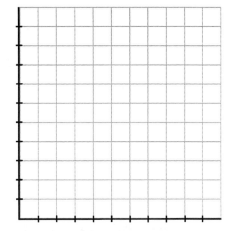

27

Law of Increasing Costs

The imaginary society of Baghina produces only two items: hot dogs and bicycles. In the table below, a certain amount of bicycles can be manufactured when a certain amount of hot dogs are manufactured, and no more of either can be produced.

Hot Dogs	Bicycles
100	0
90	4
75	8
50	12
0	16

28

What is the opportunity cost, in terms of hot dogs, for producing 8 bicycles? How much for 12 bicycles? Explain your answer and how it relates to the law of increasing costs.

Unemployment of Resources

The imaginary society of Baghina produces only two items: hot dogs and bicycles. Look at the graph of Baghina's production possibilities curve below. If some resources in Baghina are unemployed, where might the output for Baghina's production appear on the graph? Draw your answer on the graph below.

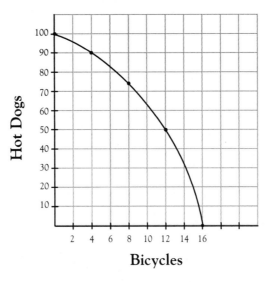

Bicycles

Can you think of a resource that is not completely employed in the United States? Why do you think this happens? Explain your answer.

© 2006 Walch Publishing

Curve Shift

The imaginary society of Baghina produces only two items: hot dogs and bicycles. On the graph below, show what would happen to Baghina's production possibilities graph if a technological change improved production across the board.

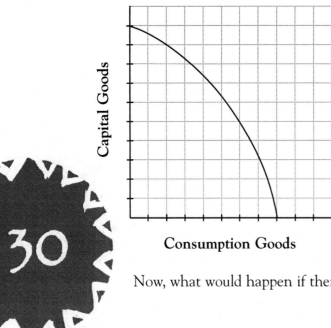

Consumption Goods

30

Now, what would happen if there was a sudden decrease in available labor?

Catastrophic Change

Hurricane Katrina destroyed the infrastructure of New Orleans, as well as other parts of the Gulf Coast. Industries were destroyed, and many people lost their lives. Those who did survive, although willing to work, did not have jobs to go to.

What effect do you suppose this disaster had on the production possibilities curve for New Orleans? In your opinion, what sort of goods should firms in New Orleans concentrate on producing, consumer goods or capital goods? Explain your opinion.

31

Economic Growth

As shown in the graphs below, the societies of Baghina and Xpatria have chosen to produce differently. Baghina has decided to produce more capital goods than Xpatria, although their production possibilities are similar. How will their curves look ten years from now? Draw your answers on the charts.

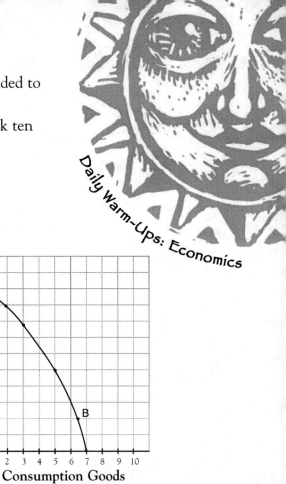

32

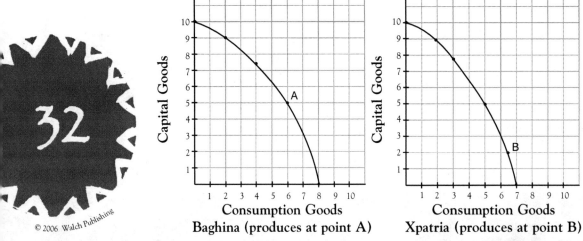

Baghina (produces at point A)

Xpatria (produces at point B)

What Would You Do?

Imagine the following: The society of Baghina is capable of producing 8 loaves of bread and harvesting 4 avocados in a day's work. The society of Xpatria can also produce 8 loaves of bread, but it can harvest 10 avocados. Here is a table of their production:

Production from 8 hours' work

	Bread	Avocados
Baghina	8	4
Xpatria	8	10

Would the countries benefit from specialization? If so, how? Explain your answer below.

33

Comparative Advantage

Imagine the following: The society of Baghina is capable of producing 8 loaves of bread and harvesting 4 avocados in a day's work. The society of Xpatria can also produce 8 loaves of bread, but it can 10 ten avocados. Here is a table of their production:

Production from 8 hours' work

	Bread	Avocados
Baghina	8	4
Xpatria	8	10

Does Baghina have a comparative advantage over Xpatria? Does Xpatria have an economic advantage over Baghina? Does opportunity cost play a role? Explain your answer below.

34

Trade Costs

Explain the following costs that are associated with trade. Use an example for each in your explanation of it.

1. transaction costs _____

   _____

   _____

2. transportation costs _____

   _____

   _____

3. artificial barriers to trade _____

   _____

   _____

35

Cost Versus Price

Imagine that you are shopping for school clothes for a new school year. You go to the mall to do your shopping. Besides the money you spend on the actual clothes, there are costs that occur for you because of your visit to the mall. What are some of these costs? Write them below, and explain why they are costs.

36

Law of Demand Vocabulary

Match each term with its definition. Write the correct letter on the line.

___ 1. law of demand

___ 2. equilibrium

___ 3. normal goods

___ 4. substitute goods

___ 5. complementary goods

a. As income increases, these goods are bought in larger amounts (and vice versa).

b. The price of a product is inversely related to the quantity demanded.

c. Closely related goods: An increase in price for one will lead to an increase in demand for the other (and vice versa).

d. Closely related goods: An increase in price for one will lead to a decrease in demand for the other (and vice versa).

e. Quantity demanded and quantity supplied are equal at this price.

37

Law of Demand

Imagine the following scenario: The price of a new CD is presently $17. You are willing to buy 2 CDs per month at that price. Your friend Leo, a big music fan, is willing to buy 5 CDs per month at that price. Your other friend, Sonia, will not pay $17 for a CD. Even though she prefers the sound quality of CDs, she decides to download music rather than pay a price of $17, even for just 1 CD.

Now, imagine that the price of CDs goes down to $15 each, and every other factor remains the same *(ceteris paribus)*. Write another scenario for you and your two friends that illustrates the law of demand.

38

Consumer Demand Schedules

The table below shows the number of CDs that you and your friend Leo are willing to buy at different prices. Using the tables, draw the individual demand graphs for you and Leo.

You

Price	Quantity
17	0
15	2
11	6
9	8
1	16

Leo

Price	Quantity
20	0
15	5
10	10
5	15
1	19

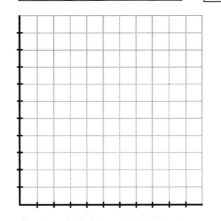

Factors of Demand

What are some of the factors that may affect a consumer's demand curve for a given product? Make a list of factors below, and describe why each may have an effect.

40

Market Demand

To determine market demand for a product, the individual demand curves for everyone in a society are added together. Using the data in the table, graph the demand curve for CDs in the society of Baghina.

Price	Quantity
20	1,000
15	2,000
10	3,000
5	4,000
1	4,800

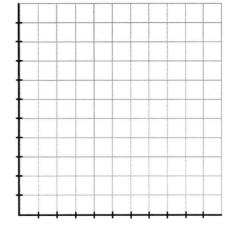

41

Attaining Equilibrium

Imagine the following scenario: At a farmers' market, every farmer is selling zucchini. As the day starts, every farmer is selling zucchini at $5 each. The market only happens once per week, and a farmer must sell what has been harvested each week before it spoils. This week, all farmers have brought a total of 300 zucchini.

Here is the neighborhood demand schedule for zucchini:

Price	Quantity
5	0
4	100
3	200
2	300
1	400

42

What should the farmers do? Explain the concept of equilibrium price in your answer.

Equilibrium Price

In a short paragraph, explain the significance of equilibrium price relative to the demand and supply for a given good. Why does having a supply below or above the equilibrium price lead to market inefficiency? How do prices settle at equilibrium? Write your answer in the space below.

43

Market-Day, Short-Run, and Long-Run Supply

The following table shows the supply of zucchini at the farmers' market in the country of Baghina for one market day, for the short run, and for the long run. Draw the three supply curves on the graph below.

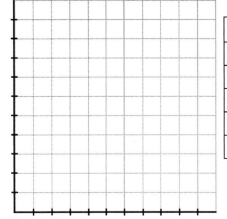

44

Price	Market day	Short run	Long run
$5	500	700	1,000
$4	500	600	750
$3	500	500	500
$2	500	400	250
$1	500	300	0

A Change in Taste

The graph below shows the demand curve for zucchini. Imagine that a widely publicized report comes out saying that zucchini is a new "superfood." What could be a new demand curve for zucchini? Draw it on the graph below.

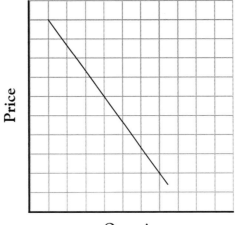

A Change in Income

Imagine that the people who regularly go to the farmers' market in the country of Baghina experience an increase in income due to an economic upturn. The original demand curve for zucchini is shown below. Draw a new demand curve showing the effect of higher incomes.

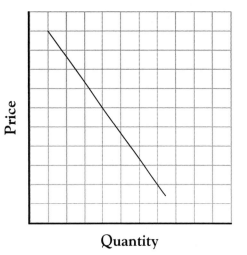

Quantity

46

The change in demand shows that zucchini is a *normal good*. Write a sentence explaining what a normal good is. Then describe a good that is not a normal good, and explain why it is not.

Substitute Goods and Complement Goods

Imagine that in the country of Baghina, the price of zucchini goes up at the farmers' market, with everything else staying equal.

1. What will happen to the demand for zucchini?

   _____

2. What will happen to the demand for substitute goods?

   _____

3. Name five substitute goods for zucchini. (*Note:* A substitute must be reasonable. Chocolate ice cream is not a substitute for zucchini!)

   _____

   _____

4. For the people at the farmers' market, zucchini isn't the same unless it's sautéed with mushrooms. In terms of zucchini, mushrooms are what type of good? _____

5. What will happen to the demand for mushrooms if the price of zucchini goes up?

   _____

47

Changes in Quantity

In a paragraph, explain the difference between a change in demand and a change in quantity demanded. Use the grid below to illustrate your explanation.

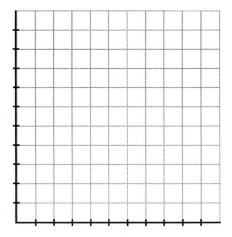

48

Change in Supply

At the farmers' market in the country of Baghina, there is a demand and supply schedule for zucchini as shown in the table. Graph the supply and demand curves below.

Price	Demand	Supply
$5	200	800
$4	300	700
$3	400	600
$2	500	500
$1	600	400

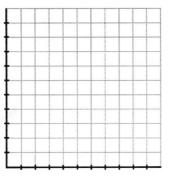

Now, what would happen to the supply curve if the amount of zucchini produced dropped due to a zucchini mold? Show the change on the graph. What has happened to the equilibrium price?

49

© 2006 Walch Publishing

Change in Resource Good

Imagine that for a new season, the price of zucchini seed is very low. What will happen to the supply curve of zucchini? What will happen to the equilibrium price of zucchini? Write your explanation, and illustrate it using the grid below.

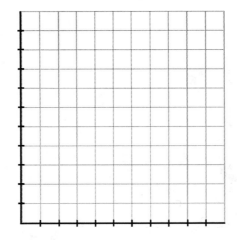

Cause and Effect

For each of the following causes, write the effect that will occur in the market. You may assume that everything else stays the same (*ceteris paribus*), and that the good in question is a normal good.

Cause	Effect
1. Demand increases.	Quantity _____.
2. Supply increases.	Price _____.
3. Price increases.	Demand _____.
4. Prices of substitutes increase.	Demand _____.
5. Prices of complements increase.	Demand _____.
6. Prices of resources decrease.	Supply _____.

51

Organize Your Prices

Look at the graphic organizer below. Every time a box such as this one □ appears, it indicates a change in equilibrium price for the good. For each empty box, write whether the equilibrium price will increase or decrease due to the change in circumstances (*ceteris paribus*).

Good = Jeans

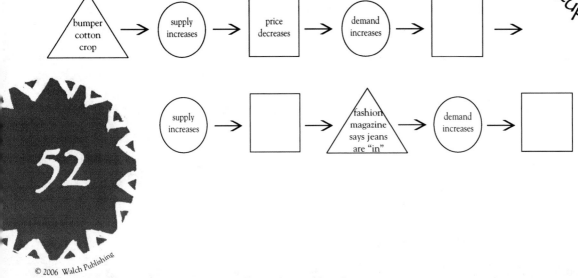

52

Equation Time

The demand curve and the supply curve for a given good are both shown as straight lines. The formula for a straight line is $y = mx + b$. For supply and demand curves, you can rewrite the formula as quantity = $b \pm m$(price).

Using the supply and demand equations below, find the equilibrium price. You can find the answer by graphing the equations, making two tables, or using algebra.

Supply: quantity = 20 + 2(price)

Demand: quantity = 40 − 2(price)

53

Substitutes: Perfect, Close, and Sort Of

Consider each pair of substitute goods below. Are they perfect substitutes, close substitutes, or just sort of substitutes for each other? By how much would an increase in price in one of the two lead to an increase in demand for the other? Explain your answers.

1. maple syrup from Maine and maple syrup from Vermont

   _____

   _____

   _____

2. Mountain Dew® and Sprite® _____

   _____

   _____

   _____

3. a movie shown in a theater and on DVD _____

   _____

   _____

54

Brand X Versus Brand Y

Imagine that there are only two different brands of potato chips on the market, Brand X and Brand Y. They taste pretty much the same, there is no difference in quality or nutritional value between the two, and they are presently offered at the same price.

Answer the following questions.

1. Can the company that makes Brand X risk raising the price of its potato chips much beyond the present price? What will happen if it does so?

2. What methods could Brand X use to make its potato chips as inelastic in demand as possible? (*Hint:* Think of strategies that lead to brand loyalty.)

55

Name That Curve

Below are the demand curves for three different products. Number the graphs from least elastic (1) to most elastic (3).

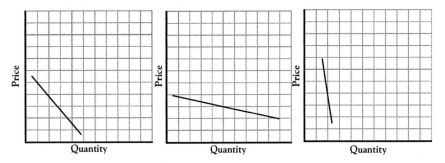

Now, list one example product for each graph, and explain your choices.

56

Personal Price Elasticity of Demand

Is there any product that, for you, price is inelastic? Name the product, and explain why you pay a wide range of prices for it.

57

Equation of Elasticity

Here is the equation for determining elasticity of demand:

$$e_d = \frac{(Q_2 - Q_1)/[(Q_2 + Q_1)/2]}{(P_2 - P_1)/[(P_2 + P_1)/2]}$$

Using a product of your choice (CDs, zucchini, shirts), write a short paragraph explaining this equation, what each term means, and how the terms relate to one another.

58

Price Elasticity of Demand

If you looked at a graph of a demand curve and saw that it was completely vertical (parallel to the y-axis), what would you say about price elasticity of demand? How about if the curve was completely horizontal (parallel to the x-axis)? Explain your answers below.

59

More Elasticity

Here is the equation for elasticity of demand:

$$e_d = \frac{(Q_2 - Q_1)/[(Q_2 + Q_1)/2]}{(P_2 - P_1)/[(P_2 + P_1)/2]}$$

Imagine that the equilibrium price of zucchini is $2. The price increases to $3 toward the end of the season, when less zucchini is brought to market. At $2, the quantity of zucchini demanded is 500. At $3, the quantity demanded is 250. Calculate the price elasticity of demand for zucchini at this price range.

60

Pricing Choices

Farmer Sutomi wants to increase the price of one of the products she brings to the farmers' market so that she can increase her revenues. But she is concerned that an increase in price for any product may drive down demand enough that she will actually lose revenue. Help her decide which of the following two products would generate more revenue if she increases its market price. Explain your answer.

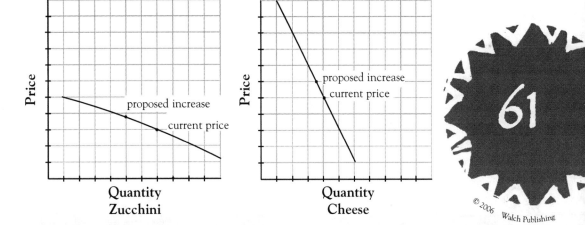

61

Short-Run and Long-Run Elasticity

Economists know that price elasticity of demand for a product is different in the long run compared to the short run. Imagine that the price of coffee increased dramatically because of a poor growing season. How would its short-run price elasticity of demand compare with its long-run price elasticity of demand? Explain your answer.

62

Elasticity Vocabulary

Match each term in the left column with a term in the right column. Write the correct letter on the line.

___ 1. unit elastic

___ 2. price elastic

___ 3. price inelastic

___ 4. income elastic

___ 5. income inelastic

a. $e_d < 1$

b. $e_d = 1$

c. For a given product, demand does not change when income changes.

d. $e_d > 1$

e. For a given product, demand does change when income changes.

63

Inferior Goods

Define what economists mean by the term *inferior good*. How are inferior goods related to income? Can you list some goods that a household would likely *not* buy as much of if its income increased? Explain your answer.

64

Elasticity and Taxes

Below are the demand curves for two products. Assume that the products sell the same quantity at their current equilibrium prices. If you were the mayor of a city and needed to raise taxes, which of these two products would you tax? Why? Explain your answer in terms of elasticity of demand.

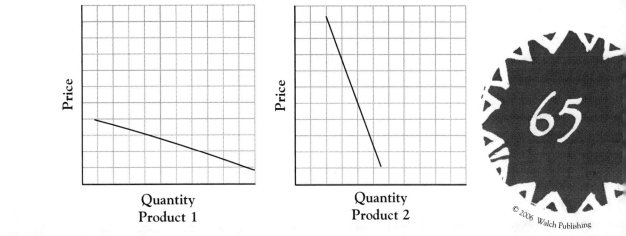

Quantity
Product 1

Quantity
Product 2

65

Prices and Price Elasticity of Demand

How is price elasticity of demand related to price? Write your answer in a paragraph. (*Hint:* Compare the price of a candy bar to the price of a house.)

66

Utility Vocabulary

Define the following terms related to utility. Use examples.

1. util

   _____

   _____

2. utility

   _____

   _____

3. marginal utility

   _____

   _____

4. total utility

   _____

   _____

67

Thinking of Utils

If you had to explain the idea of a util to someone who has never studied economics, how would you describe it? Would you place a monetary value on it? Would you compare it to something else? Write a paragraph explaining what you think a util is.

68

Diminishing Marginal Utility

Marjorie really loves peanut brittle. She gets a great deal of utility from munching it. Below is a schedule of the total utility Marjorie receives from boxes of peanut brittle over one week.

Boxes	Total Utils
1	7
2	12
3	15

How does this schedule display the law of diminishing marginal utility? How does the law relate to total utility? Explain your answers.

Total Utility Curve

Everyone knows that Marjorie loves peanut brittle. So, for her birthday, she receives a total of six boxes of peanut brittle from friends and family. She has the following utility schedule for the peanut brittle she received. Graph Marjorie's total utility curve.

70

Boxes	Total Utils
0	0
1	7
2	12
3	15
4	16
5	16
6	15

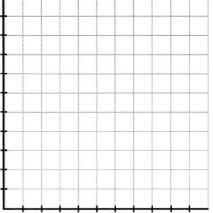

Marginal Utility Curve

Everyone knows that Marjorie loves peanut brittle. So, for her birthday, she receives a total of six boxes of peanut brittle from friends and family. She has the following utility schedule for the peanut brittle she received. Graph Marjorie's marginal utility curve.

Boxes	Total Utils
0	0
1	7
2	12
3	15
4	16
5	16
6	15

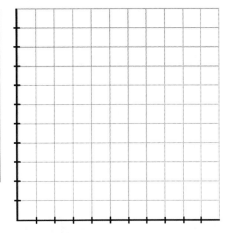

71

Noted Exceptions

The law of diminishing marginal utility applies to most things in life for most people, but it doesn't apply to everything. In a paragraph, describe a situation for you in which the law of diminishing marginal utility does not apply.

72

Budgeting Utility

Imagine that you are given $100 to spend on goods of your choice. How will you spend it? Write a list of the goods you would buy and how much you would budget for each.

How do your choices reflect principles of marginal utility over price (MU/P)?

MU/P

Imagine that you have a certain marginal utility schedule for a particular good. Your *MU/P* for that good increases as price decreases. Let's say that the good decreases in price from $10 per unit to $8 per unit. Explain what happens to the following in terms of your marginal utility for that particular good.

1. the quantity of the good you demand

   _____

   _____

   _____

74

2. the quantities you demand of other goods (*ceteris paribus*)

   _____

   _____

   _____

MU/P and Demand

In a paragraph, explain the relationship between marginal utility and the law of demand. How are the two related, and what role does price play?

Consumer Surplus

Imagine that the market-driven equilibrium price for CDs is $10 each. Leo has a particular demand schedule for CDs, which appears below. Using the schedule, determine Leo's consumer surplus when he buys his quantity of CDs at the equilibrium price. Show your work.

Price	Quantity
16	1
14	2
12	3
10	4
8	5

76

Value of a Dollar

Marginal utility is closely related to prices and to personal income. Is the value of a dollar different for different people? Explain your answer below.

77

Pricing Vocabulary

Below are some terms that refer to various forms of price control.
Write a definition of each term, and provide an example.

1. price ceiling _____

   _____

2. price floor _____

   _____

78

3. parity pricing _____

   _____

4. target pricing _____

   _____

Price Ceiling

In a paragraph, explain what a price ceiling is and why price ceilings are created and enforced.

79

Price Ceiling and Rationing

Think of what happens when a price ceiling is instituted for a particular good. What happens to the supply of the good and society's demand for it? How are price ceilings related to rationing? Explain your answer.

80

Rent Control

One of the most obvious examples of a price ceiling is rent control for a particular community. In New York City, for example, rent control was put in place because rent had become so high that low- and middle-income people could not afford it.

Imagine that two New Yorkers are discussing rent control. They argue for rent control or against rent control, taking the stance stated in parentheses. One of them is a high-school teacher (equity). The other is a landlord (market efficiency). Write each person's argument for or against rent control.

81

© 2006 Walch Publishing

Price Ceilings, Supply, and Demand

Below are the supply and demand curves for a particular good. The equilibrium price for this good is $3. Suppose there is a sudden decrease in supply to the extent that the equilibrium price shifts to $5. Since this is beyond what many can afford, society sets a price ceiling of the original equilibrium price of $3.

Daily Warm-Ups: Economics

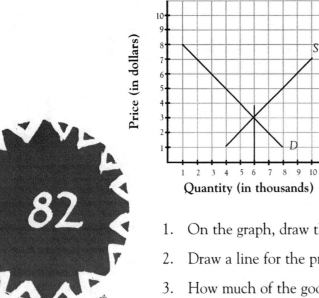

82

1. On the graph, draw the new supply curve. Label it S_1.

2. Draw a line for the price ceiling at $3. Label it P_e.

3. How much of the good can be supplied at the price ceiling? _____

Pricing Problems

What are some of the problems that can arise due to the application of a price ceiling on a good? Think of an example of a price ceiling to help you explain your answer.

Price Floor

In a paragraph, explain what a price floor is and why price floors are created and enforced.

84

Excess Supply

How is a price floor for a particular product related to excess supply? What happens to the excess supply of a good under a price floor? Explain your answer, remembering how the supply and demand curves for a product function to settle at equilibrium.

85

© 2006 Walch Publishing

Price Floors, Supply, and Demand

Below is a graph of the supply and demand curves for a particular good. The equilibrium price of the good is $3. Suppose there is a sudden increase in supply for the good, such that the supply curve shifts to a new equilibrium price of $1. A price floor is instituted at the old equilibrium price of $3.

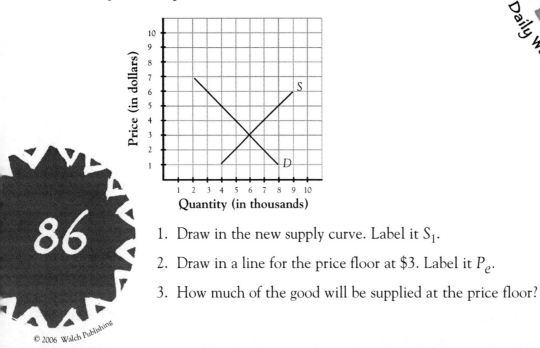

86

1. Draw in the new supply curve. Label it S_1.

2. Draw in a line for the price floor at $3. Label it P_e.

3. How much of the good will be supplied at the price floor?

Types of Businesses

Write a short description of each type of business below. Briefly state the advantages and disadvantages of each.

1. sole proprietorship _____
   _____
   _____
   _____

2. partnership _____
   _____
   _____
   _____

3. corporation _____
   _____
   _____
   _____

87

Liability

In a paragraph, explain the difference between unlimited liability and limited liability. To what types of companies does each apply?

88

Here's a Start

The paragraph below is about the founding of a particular type of business. There are some words missing, however. Fill in the missing words to complete the paragraph.

Owen is the _____ (the only owner) of a thriving chain of bicycle stores. He decides to form a(n) _____, which will be its own legal unit. This will allow Owen to change his _____ from unlimited to limited. First, Owen obtains a(n) _____. This is a legal document from his state creating this new type of business. Then he issues shares of his new company's _____.

89

Types of Stocks

Match the type of stock on the left with its description on the right. Write the correct letter on the line.

___ 1. common stock

___ 2. preferred stock

___ 3. convertible stock

a. fixed dividend; no voting rights

b. yields dividends based on performance; voting rights

c. fixed dividend; voting rights; can be changed to common stock

Now, describe the difference between shares of stock and corporate bonds.

_____

_____

_____

Cost Vocabulary

Match each term with its definition. Write the correct letter on the line.

_____ 1. fixed cost

_____ 2. variable cost

_____ 3. average total cost

_____ 4. average fixed cost

_____ 5. average variable cost

_____ 6. marginal cost

a. the total cost divided by quantity

b. a cost that is the same regardless of quantity produced

c. a cost that changes depending on quantity produced

d. the total fixed cost divided by quantity

e. the added cost from one more unit of production

f. the total variable cost divided by quantity

Daily Warm-Ups: Economics

Fixed Cost

Imagine that you wish to go into one of the following businesses. What sort of fixed costs might you encounter to start your business? Choose one business, and write a list of all the fixed costs that might be required to enter into it.

farming

owning a donut shop

publishing a magazine

being an electrician

owning a commercial fishing business

92

Fixed Versus Variable

In a paragraph, describe the difference between a fixed cost and a variable cost. Use examples of each in your explanation.

93

Law of Diminishing Returns

In a paragraph, describe the law of diminishing returns. What part do fixed costs play? Does the law only apply to labor?

94

Fixed Cost Versus Law of Diminishing Returns

In a paragraph, explain what effect (in terms of fixed costs) an investment in a firm has on the law of diminishing returns. What part does technology play in the dynamic between investment and returns?

95

Name Those Initials

Economics uses a vast array of initials and acronyms. These can sometimes be confusing. Below are a group of initials associated with the costs of production. For each, say what the initials stand for.

1. TC _____

2. TFC _____

3. TVC _____

4. ATC _____

5. AFC _____

6. AVC _____

7. MC _____

96

Identify the Expression

Match each expression on the left with what it equals on the right. Write the correct letter on the line. You will use one letter more than once.

___ 1. TC/Q

___ 2. TFC/Q

___ 3. TVC/Q

___ 4. TFC + TVC

___ 5. AFC + AVC

a. AFC

b. AVC

c. ATC

d. TC

97

Table of Costs 1

Below is a table of total costs for a particular company. Complete the table, and graph the *TC*, *TFC*, and *TVC* curves on the grid.

98

Q	TFC	TVC	TC
0	$100	$0	
1		$50	
2		$70	
3		$80	
4		$95	
5		$130	

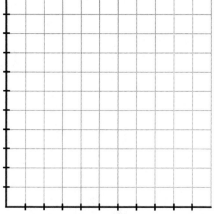

Table of Costs II

Below is a table of total costs for a particular company. Complete the table, and then convert the data to find AFC, AVC, ATC, and MC. Create a new table to display the data.

Q	TFC	TVC	TC
0	$100	$0	
1		$50	
2		$70	
3		$80	
4		$95	
5		$130	

99

AFC Curve

Below is a graph of an average fixed cost curve.

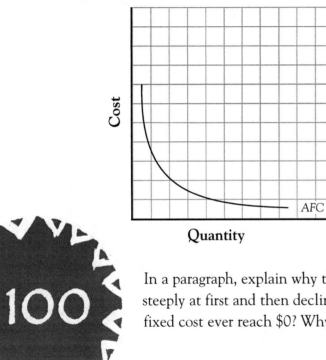

100

In a paragraph, explain why the cost curve is shaped the way it is—declining steeply at first and then declining gradually as P reaches $0. Will the average fixed cost ever reach $0? Why or why not?

AVC Curve

Below is a typical average variable cost curve. You can see that it is U-shaped. In a short paragraph, explain why the curve is shaped this way.

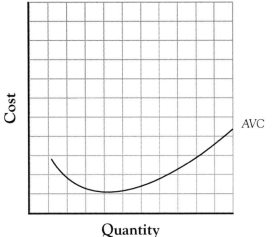

Implicit and Explicit Costs

Below is a list of costs Jose incurred when he left his employment as a chef and began a basket-weaving business from his home. For each cost, say whether it is implicit or explicit.

1. cost of basket-weaving materials _____

2. cost of use of Jose's spare room as a basket-weaving studio
   _____

3. cost of accountant for business record-keeping _____

4. cost of Jose leaving his job as a chef _____

5. cost of Jose cashing a matured CD as start-up money _____

102

Daily Warm-Ups: Economics

Marginal Cost

The graph below shows a typical *ATC* curve and a typical MC curve superimposed. Look at the graph, and answer the questions that follow.

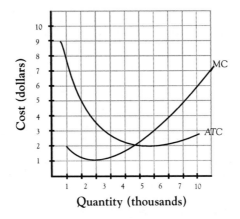

1. When MC is less than *ATC*, is *ATC* rising or declining?

   _____

2. When MC is more than *ATC*, is *ATC* rising or declining?

   _____

103

Marginal Cost Calculation

Using the formula MC = ΔTC/ΔQ, complete the following table.

Q	ΔQ	TC	ΔTC	MC
0	0	$1,000	0	N/A
100	100	$1,150		$1.50
200		$1,280		
300		$1,395		
400		$1,505		
500		$1,610		
600		$1,710		
700		$1,825		
800		$1,975		
900		$2,185		
1,000		$2,465		

Daily Warm-Ups: Economics

104

Revenue

Match each expression on the left with what it equals on the right. Write the correct letter on the line.

_____ 1. PQ

_____ 2. TR/Q

_____ 3. $\Delta TR/\Delta Q$

a. marginal revenue

b. total revenue

c. average revenue (also P)

105

MC and MR

The graph below shows the MC and MR curves for a certain product from a particular firm. Calculate the marginal cost/revenue for points A, B, and C.

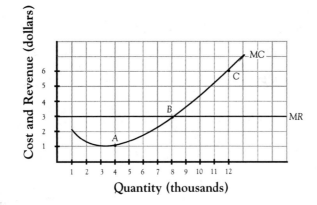

106

At what point should the firm produce?

Market Definition

Below is a list of some products. Some of them have cross elasticities that are relatively high, while others may be less related. Remember that products with a high cross elasticity belong to the same or a similar market.

Organize the products into the graphic organizer below.

zucchini

squashes

vegetables

automobiles

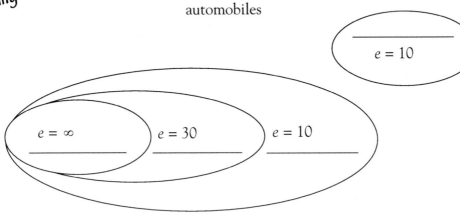

$e = 10$

$e = \infty$

$e = 30$

$e = 10$

107

Market Structure

Describe each of the following types of market structure. Specify the relative number of firms in each type.

1. monopoly _____

    _____

2. oligopoly _____

    _____

3. monopolistic competition _____

    _____

    4. perfect competition _____

    _____

108

The Ideal Market

To make economic modeling easier, economists have developed the concept of the ideal market. This market does not truly exist anywhere, but it has four features that markets strive to achieve. List and describe these features.

109

Oligopoly and Cartel Pricing

In a paragraph, explain how the existence of an oligopoly can lead to a cartel and cartel pricing. Give an example of a cartel.

110

Natural Monopoly

In a natural monopoly, the costs of another firm entering the market are so high compared to the existing firm's marginal cost, no other firm wishes to enter.

List an example of a natural monopoly. What features of the product in question lead the market structure to be monopolistic? Explain your answer.

111

Monopoly Pricing

Many people assume that when a monopoly exists, the single firm will put whatever price on its product that it wants—specifically, a really high price. Is this truly the case? Explain your answer, keeping in mind the rule of $MR = MC$.

112

Entering the Market

At the farmers' market this summer, Holly is the single seller of Thai basil. It sells quite well. There is a high demand for Thai basil among the consumers at the farmers' market.

Seeing how well Holly has done, several other farmers from the farmers' market will grow and sell Thai basil next summer. Answer the following questions.

1. What two things will happen to the demand curve for Holly's Thai basil?

   _____

   _____

2. What will happen to Holly's profits for Thai basil? _____

   _____

3. What will likely happen to the price of Thai basil at the market?

   _____

   _____

113

Perfect Competition

In a paragraph, describe the features of perfect competition. Why is perfect competition desirable? How does it lead to efficiency in the market?

114

Intervention in Monopoly

Imagine that a monopoly exists in the cell-phone service industry. Only one company serves all cell-phone users. Suddenly, it is discovered that the cell-phone company is on the verge of bankruptcy—providing service for cell phones is not as profitable as everyone thought!

Should the government intervene and bail out the cell-phone company? Why or why not? Explain your answer.

Intervention in Market

In your opinion, should government ever take over industries that are struggling? Choose one of the industries listed below. These are all industries that a government of the United States (federal, state, or local) has taken over. In a paragraph, explain why the takeover occurred, even when the takeover would likely never lead to a profitable enterprise. Why would government want to see the service provided?

1. rail (train) service

2. garbage collection

3. health services

116

Large Companies

Much antitrust (anti-monopolistic) legislation in the United States over the years has focused on very large companies that have a disproportionately large share of a market. Think of a large company. List some of the ways in which this company protects and enlarges its market share.

117

© 2006 Walch Publishing

Regulation of Monopoly

Imagine that a telephone (landline) company exists in a community. It is the only company that provides landline telephone service. Anyone who wants telephone service in the community must pay this company. The company determines it can make its highest profit if it charges $45 per month and serves 100,000 of the community's 200,000 households. (In other words, along the demand curve, half of the community's households are willing to pay that price for service.)

The community government wants significantly more than half of the community to have landline phone service. What should they do? Explain your answer in terms of price and cost of service.

118

Demand for Labor

Look at the following schedule for labor demanded by a firm, alongside the firm's marginal revenue. Each new hire costs the company $20. Calculate the difference between marginal revenue (MRP) and marginal cost of labor (MCL). How many people will the firm hire?

Laborers	MRP	MCL	MRP-MCL
0	—	—	
1	$30	$20	
2	$36	$20	
3	$40	$20	
4	$32	$20	
5	$28	$20	
6	$20	$20	
7	$16	$20	
8	$10	$20	

119

© 2006 Walch Publishing

Minimum Wage

There are many good arguments as to why there should be a minimum wage established by law. Many economists and legislators, however, argue against a minimum wage. What is their argument? Explain it, and describe how the supply curve for labor and the marginal revenue of companies factor in.

120

Outsourcing

Many people feel that the establishment of a minimum wage has caused U.S. companies to turn to foreign labor markets to "buy" their labor. Also, retailers often buy goods for resale that are made cheaply by low-paid workers in foreign countries. Some economists feel that the minimum wage should be abolished in the United States for this reason. Rather than pay the higher wages, companies will simply buy their labor elsewhere.

Do you think the minimum wage should be abolished? Why or why not? Explain your answer.

121

Monopsony

In a paragraph, describe the relationship between monopsony and unionization. How does the dynamic between monopsony and labor function?

122

Wealth

In a paragraph, describe what *wealth* is. How is it different from income? What constitutes wealth besides money? How can income generate wealth, and vice versa?

123

Difference in Income

The gap between the richest and the poorest in U.S. society has been getting larger over the past few decades. Do you think this is fair? Should government regulation intervene to try to close up this gap? If so, in what ways? Explain your answer.

124

Poverty

There are two different ways to measure poverty. One is to calculate average income for a given country and decide on a poverty threshold that is a certain percentage of that income. The other way is to establish a minimum standard of living that all people in a society should be able to achieve and determine the cost of that living.

What are the advantages and disadvantages of each method? Which method do you think creates a more workable definition of poverty? Which one would be better for comparing U.S. poverty with that in other countries? Explain your answer.

125

© 2006 Walch Publishing

Welfare

In your opinion, does welfare truly help poor people or merely hinder them? Explain your answer.

126

Tax Vocabulary

The words in the box have something to do with taxation in the United States. Match each word in the box with its definition below. Write the correct letter on the line.

a.	excise	c.	progressive	e.	recessive
b.	exempt	d.	proportional	f.	tariff

___ 1. a fee placed on an import

___ 2. not required to pay tax

___ 3. a tax levied on manufactured goods and on services

___ 4. type of tax in which the tax rate increases as income increases

___ 5. type of tax in which the tax rate stays the same over all incomes

___ 6. type of tax in which the tax rate increases as income decreases

127

Types of Taxes

Listed below are three different types of taxes. Explain how each type works, and give an example of a tax that fits that type.

1. progressive _____

_____

_____

_____

2. regressive _____

_____

_____

_____

3. proportional _____

_____

_____

_____

128

Direct Versus Hidden

In a paragraph, explain the difference between a direct tax and a hidden tax.

129

Tariffs

What is a tariff? How is it similar to a tax? In what way are tariffs related to tax shifts? Explain your answer.

130

Income Tax

Economists and legislators disagree about how income should be taxed. Some argue for a flat tax, or proportional tax. Others argue for a progressive income tax. What is the difference between these two types of income tax? What are the arguments for and against each type? Explain your answer.

131

Taxation and Equity

Why would a government be willing to levy a 20% tax on a luxury item, such as a yacht, but refrain from taxing everyday items, such as food and medicine? Do you believe this is fair? Explain why or why not.

132

Taxation and Social Issues

Governments typically levy a "sin" tax on items such as cigarettes and alcohol. Read the scenario below, and then answer the questions that follow.

Rosario and Dylan both smoke two packs of cigarettes a day. They are the same age. Rosario grew up in a wealthy household, went to private schools, attended college, and now works at a job paying $150,000 per year. Dylan grew up in a poor household, could not afford college, and went to work at a low-paying job right after high school. He works for $25,000 per year.

1. Governments establish sin taxes for two reasons: inelasticity of demand and deterrence. Explain.

2. Are sin taxes fair? Why or why not?

133

© 2006 Walch Publishing

GDP and Growth Vocabulary

Match each term on the left with its definition on the right. Write the correct letter on the line.

_____ 1. GDP (gross domestic product)

_____ 2. nominal GDP

_____ 3. real GDP

_____ 4. CPI (consumer price index)

_____ 5. aggregate supply

_____ 6. aggregate demand

a. method of comparing the prices of goods and services in a given year to a base year

b. all the goods and services in an economy that firms are willing to supply at different prices

c. the value of all the goods and services produced in a given year

d. all of the goods and services that people in a given economy demand

e. GDP measured in current prices

f. GDP measured after being adjusted for price changes

134

Macro Vocabulary

The following terms have something to do with the functioning of the economy of the United States. Match each term on the left with its definition on the right. Write the correct letter on the line.

_____ 1. recession

_____ 2. depression

_____ 3. inflation

_____ 4. trough

_____ 5. recovery

_____ 6. peak

_____ 7. downturn

a. an increase in price level

b. the highest point of a business cycle

c. a decline in GDP for at least six months

d. the lowest point of a business cycle

e. a long-term, severe recession

f. a period of declining GDP and increasing unemployment

g. a period of increasing GDP and decreasing unemployment

135

CPI

The consumer price index (CPI) is a measure comparing the prices of goods and services commonly purchased in a base year to the prices of those same goods and services in a future year. For instance, a shopping basket full of goods bought in 1997 (the base year) might be less expensive than those same goods purchased in 2000. The comparison can help determine how prices have changed over time.

If you were creating your own personal CPI, what sorts of goods would be in your shopping basket? Make a list of items you most typically spend your money on. Do you think these items will go up or down in years to come?

136

GDP

Economists determine gross domestic product in two different ways. These are listed below. Describe each method of calculation and what it includes.

1. expenditure approach _____

   _____

   _____

   _____

2. income approach _____

   _____

   _____

   _____

137

GDP, Nominal and Real

In a paragraph, explain the difference between nominal GDP and real GDP. How is real GDP calculated?

138

Aggregate Supply

The following graph shows aggregate supply for the United States in a particular time period. At what point along the curve does full employment occur?

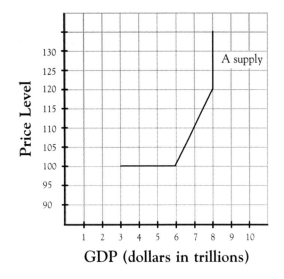

Wartime Prosperity

Often in U.S. history, a depression, recession, or economic downturn comes to an end due to U.S. entrance into a war. Explain this phenomenon in terms of aggregate supply and aggregate demand.

140

Tax-Cut Prosperity

One way in which economists and legislators try to stimulate a sluggish economy is by cutting taxes. These tax cuts are often for people who already have significant discretionary income. What argument do lawmakers put forth to justify cutting taxes in this way? Explain the theory in terms of aggregate supply and aggregate demand.

141

Full Employment Versus Inflation

Explain, in terms of aggregate supply, why it is difficult to have full employment and low inflation simultaneously.

142

Calculating GDP

Explain the difference between intermediate goods and final goods. Why are intermediate goods not counted when determining GDP?

143

NDP

How is NDP calculated from GDP? How is national income then calculated? In a paragraph, explain the progression from GDP to national income.

144

Zero Growth

Early economists thought that the growth rate of the economy would eventually reach zero. They thought that as the means of production were used up, the economy would simply not be able to grow further. They did not take into account the incredible opportunities created by technology.

How do advances in technology guarantee economic growth? Explain your answer.

145

Underground Economy

Aside from criminal activity, such as the sale of illegal drugs, there is a thriving underground economy in the United States. What are some examples of this underground economy? Name and describe three examples.

146

Theorists of Consumption

Match each economist on the left with his theory of consumer behavior on the right. Write the correct letter on the line.

_____ 1. Keynes

_____ 2. Duesenberry

_____ 3. Friedman

_____ 4. Modigliani

a. permanent income hypothesis

b. life-cycle hypothesis

c. absolute income hypothesis

d. relative income hypothesis

Theories of Consumption

Match each theory of consumption with its description. Write the correct letter on the line.

_____ 1. absolute income hypothesis

_____ 2. relative income hypothesis

_____ 3. permanent income hypothesis

_____ 4. life-cycle hypothesis

a. Consumption changes depending on whether people are just starting out, nearing retirement, and so forth.

b. Marginal consumption increases at a constant rate as income increases.

c. Long-term income, rather than fluctuations in income, dictates consumption.

d. Consumption increases, by diminishing amounts, as income increases.

Autonomous Consumption

What is autonomous consumption? Why is it an important issue to consider when examining issues of consumption and income in the United States? Explain your answer.

149

Unemployment

In a paragraph, explain how the federal Bureau of Labor Statistics defines unemployment. Whom does it include and exclude from its definition, and why? Do you think the definition is adequate?

150

The Mattress Principle

You have probably heard of people who are afraid of putting money in the bank. This fear is likely a legacy of the bank failures that occurred during the Great Depression. Some of these people hid cash in their mattresses or a similar hiding place. Explain why, in spite of hiding it so carefully, these people actually lost money.

151

Money Vocabulary

Define the following.

1. barter _____

   _____

2. fiat money _____

   _____

3. currency _____

   _____

4. velocity of money _____

   _____

152

Barter

In a paragraph, describe the barter system. What are its advantages and disadvantages? If you had to function within a barter system, what would you produce to trade, and why?

Method of Exchange

In how many different ways do people exchange one thing of value for another? Write all of the different methods you can think of.

154

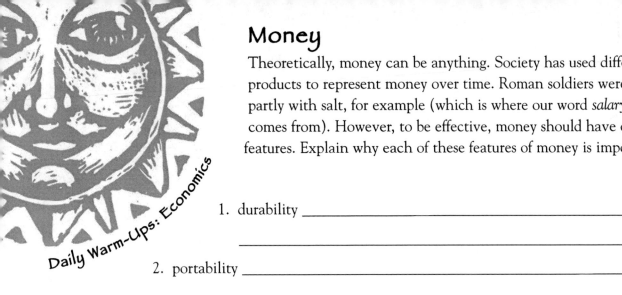

Money

Theoretically, money can be anything. Society has used different products to represent money over time. Roman soldiers were paid partly with salt, for example (which is where our word *salary* comes from). However, to be effective, money should have certain features. Explain why each of these features of money is important.

1. durability _____

_____

2. portability _____

_____

3. divisibility _____

_____

4. homogeneity _____

_____

5. stability _____

_____

155

Gold

Explain why gold became a preferred material to represent money. What are the features of gold that make it an excellent choice?

156

Fiat Money

Explain the difference between money based on a standard, such as gold or silver, and fiat money. What is the logic behind fiat money?

157

Money Today

In the space below, write all of the different denominations of currency put out by the United States today. Then answer the questions.

1. From what materials is this currency made?

   _____

   _____

158

2. Is this money? Why or why not?

   _____

   _____

   _____

   _____

Types of Money

Define the following kinds of money. Provide examples of each.

1. M1 _____

_____

_____

2. M2 _____

_____

_____

3. M3 _____

_____

_____

159

Equation of Exchange

How does the amount of money in a society affect the prices of goods? Look at the equation below.

$$MV = PQ$$

Explain the equation, stating what each term represents.

160

Banking

In a paragraph, explain why banks were established in the United States. How has the federal government regulated the banking industry? Why were these regulations needed?

161

The Reserve System

Do you have a savings account or a checking account? If so, you should know that banks are required to keep only a small portion (3% to 10%) of their deposit accounts in cash reserves. Does this make you nervous? In a paragraph, explain the reasoning behind the reserve system.

162

The Fed

The paragraph below describes the Federal Reserve System.
Choose the words in parentheses to best complete the paragraph.

The Federal Reserve System, or the Fed, is a(n) (government-owned, independent) agency that answers to (Congress, the U.S. president). The system is split into (nine, twelve) districts, each serving a particular region of the United States. Nationally chartered banks (must, can) be members of the Fed. All banks, including state-chartered banks, that are members contribute (3%, 5%) of their capital to the reserve, and a(n) (equal, larger) amount of the members' capital remains on call.

163

The Fed: Currency Creation

The Federal Reserve System, or the Fed, has several roles. One of them is the creation of paper currency.

Describe what paper currency is. What determines how much paper money is in circulation?

The Fed: Check Clearing

Imagine that you live in Maine. You decide to go on vacation in New Mexico. In Albuquerque, you eat at a restaurant called Kelly's and decide to pay with a check.

Your bank is in Maine. Kelly's bank is in New Mexico. The two banks don't have a business connection. Why does Kelly's bank accept your check? Write one or two sentences for your answer.

165

Increase in Money Supply

Imagine that the Federal Reserve System, or the Fed, increases the money supply. It has some immediate, but perhaps not long-lasting, effects.

Answer the following questions.

1. What happens to the interest rate?

   _____

   2. What happens to the aggregate demand curve?

      _____

      3. What happens to GDP?

         _____

166

Discount Rate

One of the roles of the Federal Reserve System, or the Fed, is to provide loans to banks. The interest rate on these loans is called the **discount rate.** Under what circumstances does the Fed lower its discount rate? Under what circumstances does it increase it? Explain your answer.

Unemployment and Inflation

Macroeconomists often focus on how best to stabilize the economy by reducing the unemployment rate and the rate of inflation. How are these two rates related? How do they, together, present a paradox for economists? Explain your answer.

168

Views of Unemployment

The field of economics has a variety of "schools" that view problems differently and propose different methods to handle these problems. One problem economists think about is unemployment. What solution would each of the following types of economists propose for the problem of unemployment?

1. Classical _____

   _____

   _____

2. Keynesian _____

   _____

   _____

3. Supply-side _____

   _____

   _____

169

Public Goods Versus Merit Goods

What is the difference between a public good and a merit good? Explain your answer, and give two examples of each.

170

Daily Warm-Ups: Economics

Publicly Supplied Goods

The goods listed below are generally considered to be public goods or near-public goods. Choose one good and describe why the government is a more suitable provider for this good than a private firm. Could the good be offered by a private firm under certain circumstances? Explain your answer.

a lighthouse

education

clean air

a city park

national defense

171

Transfer Payments

The U.S. government spends a certain amount of money helping people who are economically disadvantaged. Such spending is sometimes referred to as **transfer payments.** This is because the government is, in essence, transferring money from the better off to the less well off through taxation.

Give three examples of transfer payments, and state whether you think each payment is justified.

172

Social Security

In a paragraph, explain what the U.S. Social Security system is and why it was created. How does the system work in terms of gathering and disbursing funds?

173

Global Economy Vocabulary

Define the following.

1. free trade _____
   _____

2. imports _____
   _____

3. exports _____
   _____

4. reciprocity _____
   _____

5. World Trade Organization (WTO) _____
   _____

6. European Union (EU) _____
   _____

7. North American Free Trade Agreement (NAFTA) _____
   _____

174

Sweatshops

Choose one of the following roles. Develop an argument, from the point of view of the role you have chosen, about the political or economic regulation of sweatshops overseas.

the CEO of a brand-name clothing store chain

a student wishing to abolish sweatshop labor

a low-income American trying to make ends meet

175

NAFTA

The acronym NAFTA stands for North American Free Trade Agreement. What political issues did NAFTA raise in North America when it was proposed? Explain your answers in a paragraph below.

176

Explaining Tariffs

In a paragraph, explain why tariffs are placed on imports to the United States. How can tariffs affect the demand curve for identical U.S. goods?

177

The EU

The European Union, or EU, has often been in the news in recent years. Many European nations not yet in the EU want very much to join. What economic advantages are there for nations that belong to the EU? Explain your answer.

178

LDCs

In a paragraph, describe the features that identify less-developed countries (LDCs). What are some of the barriers LDCs face that inhibit their growth and keep their people in the cycle of poverty?

179

Low Income, High Birth Rate

Less-developed countries are often characterized by having low income rates and high population growth rates. Answer the following.

1. Many African countries are considered to be less-developed. Why does a high population growth rate contribute to the problem of low per capita income?

180

2. How does the AIDS pandemic affecting some of the same countries make the problem even worse?

1. Answers will vary, but responses should include examples of a social science (anthropology, psychology, political sciences, and so forth). Students should point out that a social science involves the study of people, as individuals or as groups. Since people are involved, a social science differs from a hard science because of the difficulty of pure experimentation.

2. Answers will vary. Sample answers: political science often deals in the marketing and "spin" of candidates for office, which has its base in economic thinking; sociology often looks at issues such as the effects of poverty, which are due to economic forces; history often looks at how economic forces drive political events (such as the Russian revolutions); anthropology takes into consideration the development of societies in relation to the development of markets.

3. Answers will vary.

4. Answers will vary, but it should be noted that this is a trick question. Students will be hard pressed to find anything that is truly free.

5. Answers will vary. Sample answer:

Raw materials	Information	Technology

coal
iron
oil
minerals
	bookkeeping
	market research
	customer
	   databases
	best methods of
	   production
		inventions
		improved
		   manufacturing
		   tools
		innovations in
		   material
		   processing

6. Answers may vary slightly. Here is some sample information the answer should contain: Raw materials that go into a bicycle frame include steel, aluminum, titanium, or carbon fiber. Plastics and other metals are used for other parts of the bicycle. Labor must be used to acquire this material through mining or other extraction. Then

labor must be used to refine the material for use. Technology is involved in all aspects of manufacture and sale, from the acquiring of raw material to the design, engineering, and production of the bicycle to the transaction of selling the bicycle. Information must be used by bicycle manufacturers to make the bicycle as appealing as possible to consumers. Ultimately, labor must be used to market and sell the bicycle to customers.

7. Answers will vary. Diamond, petroleum, iron, coal, titanium, and salt are all nonrenewable. Wheat, cotton, and wood are renewable, but make certain that students are aware of concerns such as depletion of soil nutrients and the problems wrought by deforestation.

8. 1. c; 2. e; 3. a; 4. d; 5. b

9. Answers will vary.

10. Answers will vary. Make certain that students understand the concept of opportunity cost. They

may not plan to spend their time doing the things they would pay themselves the most money for!

11. Answers will vary slightly. They should include: the transaction between a mine company and a landowner with a deposit of silicon; the purchase of labor and means of production by the mine owner; the sale of the silicon to a silicon chip manufacturer; the sale of the chip to a computer manufacturer; the sale of the computer to the consumer. Other answers may include subsidiary transactions, such as advertising for the computer.

12. Answers will vary. Sample answers: yard sale, grocery store, online retailer, hotel, pizza parlor, and so forth.

13. Answers will vary, but should point to the impossibility of experimental research in market behavior. The "market" is so widespread and complicated, formal experimentation is not a realistic approach. There is, however, data that supports the ideal market model of human

behavior (and, it should be pointed out, some data that does not).

14. Answers will vary. Sample answer:

Positive	Negative
ate a good breakfast, +5 points	stayed up late playing guitar, –5 points
studied hard, +10 points	didn't take very good notes, –15 points
got to class early, +2 points	forgot my favorite pen at home, –3 points

15. Answers will vary. Sample answer: Consumer: A factory may buy labor, raw materials, and fixed-cost items such as machines, new technology, and information (customer lists, trade magazines, and so forth); Producer: A factory may produce its main item for sale to retail, materials and subsidiary products for other factories, and benefits to the community such as charitable donations.

16. Answers will vary. Sample answer: The cost of health care is an issue in microeconomics in that the cost of providing it has become so expensive, fewer employers are able to provide it to their workers. This causes the price to increase even more as there are fewer people to spread the costs. This is an issue that concerns the behavior of individual people and firms. Offshoring (sending jobs overseas) is a macroeconomic issue in that it is a reflection of the wage rate and labor laws in the United States. It also has affected the nature of the U.S. job force (from manufacturing to service jobs). This is a macroeconomic issue in that it concerns the economy as a whole.

17.

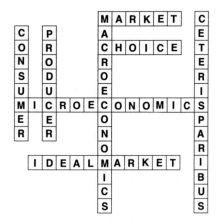

The crossword answers read:
MARKET, MACROECONOMICS, CHOICE, CONSUMER, PRODUCER, MICROECONOMICS, CETERIS PARIBUS, IDEAL MARKET

18. Answers will vary. Sample answer for the minimum wage: Positive: Under unregulated market conditions, labor is "bought" at the price the market will bear. When there is a larger supply of workers, wages tend to be low. This is the market-driven minimum wage. Normative: When the wage rate is left to settle at its market-driven level, it is usually too low for families to make a living. Families also don't have extra income to spend on goods and services, which leaves the economic growth stagnant. Therefore, government should intervene and set a minimum wage. (*Note:* The argument against setting a minimum wage, in that it leads to higher unemployment, is also acceptable.)

19. Answers will vary, but should demonstrate an understanding of rational self-interest.

20. Answers will vary slightly. In pure communism, all property and means of production, human and nonhuman, are publicly owned. In socialism, most nonhuman resources are publicly owned. Most countries these days are a mix of capitalist and communist ideas.

21. Answers will vary.

22. Answers will vary. Sample answer: I need to study for a test. The first hour I study is the most beneficial, then each half hour after that has a

benefit to me, but each half hour has marginally less benefit than the one before. Finally, I reach a point at which I am so tired, any more time spent studying begins to cost me rather than benefit me.

23. 1. b; 2. e; 3. d; 4. a; 5. c
24. Answers will vary slightly. 1. Labor is the human power that goes into the production of any product, as well as its delivery to the market, its sale, and so forth. 2. Capital is any tool used to create a good—machinery is a good example. 3. Land is a natural resource and anything arising in a natural state from that resource, such as lumber or minerals. 4. Entrepreneurship is the act of developing and producing products and services.
25. 1. d; 2. a; 3. b; 4. f; 5. e; 6. c
26. Answers will vary. Students should produce realistic alternatives to the original activity. For example, "sunbathing" would not be an appropriate alternative for a student in the Northeast in the winter.

27.

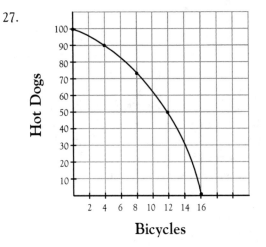

28. If 8 bicycles are produced, that means 75 hot dogs can be produced rather than 100, for an opportunity cost of 25 hot dogs. For 12 bicycles, only 50 hot dogs can be produced, for an opportunity cost of 50 hot dogs. Students should show awareness that the marginal opportunity cost

Daily Warm-Ups: Economics

in hot dogs increases as the marginal production of bicycles increases.

29. Students should draw a dot somewhere between the origin and the production possibilities curve. Other answers will vary. Students will likely think of unemployment of labor. Demand for labor may be low for a variety of reasons, such as lack of another resource (capital, for example).

30. Answers will vary slightly, but students should show first an outward movement of the curve and then an inward movement. Sample answer:

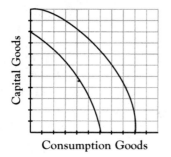

Consumption Goods

31. Answers will vary slightly, but they should state that the possibilities curve of New Orleans moves dramatically inward toward the origin. According to economic theory, New Orleans should put emphasis on capital goods in order to provide jobs and improve its infrastructure.

32.

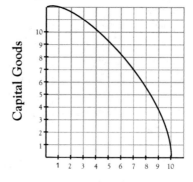

Consumption Goods
Baghina (produces at point A)

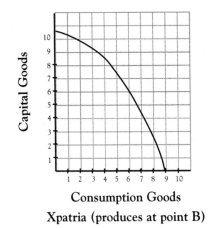

Consumption Goods

Xpatria (produces at point B)

33. The countries would benefit from specialization, since Xpatria can produce 10 avocados compared with Baghina's 4, and Baghina can produce bread at an opportunity cost of only 4 avocados compared with Xpatria's opportunity cost of 10 avocados.

34. Xpatria can produce 10 avocados compared with Baghina's 4, so Xpatria has an economic advantage over Baghina when it comes to avocados. However, Baghina can produce bread at an opportunity cost of only 4 avocados compared with Xpatria's opportunity cost of 10 avocados; thus, Baghina has a comparative advantage over Xpatria when it comes to bread.

35. Answers will vary slightly.
    1. Transaction costs occur due to the exchange of money for goods. Examples are brokers' fees, the opportunity cost or shopping, and contract fees (such as when buying a house). 2. Transportation costs occur any time there is movement of a good from one place to another. Examples are gasoline costs, refrigeration costs, and shipping costs.
    3. Artificial barriers to trade are costs imposed by a government to slow or inhibit trade. Examples are tariffs and import quotas.

36. Answers should include: the time spent traveling to and from the mall; gasoline/bus fare used in

traveling; the time waiting in line; the time trying on clothes; the cost of walking to and from different stores; time necessary for chatting with the friends encountered; food costs for snacks; and so forth. Anything is a cost when the time or resource could be spent in the next best use.

37. 1. b; 2. e; 3. a; 4. c; 5. d

38. Answers will vary, but students should answer that the number of CDs each person buys will increase. Sonia can be an exception. Since she has not shown a willingness to buy CDs, it can be argued that she won't buy CDs at $15, either.

39.

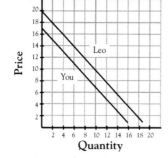

40. Income changes: More or less money to spend will affect a person's demand curve for a given product. Availability of substitutes: If there are adequate substitutes available for a product, a person will demand more or less of the product depending on price. Availability of related goods: If a product has other goods related to it, the price of the related goods will affect the demand for the product (high-priced related goods will drive down demand, and vice versa).

41.

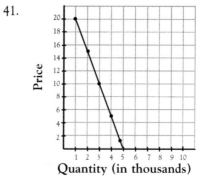

42. The farmers should lower their price to $2 per zucchini. This is the point at which they can sell off their zucchini at the most beneficial price for them and at which they will not run out of supply. This is also the price at which demand will settle and is thus the equilibrium price.

43. Answers will vary. Sample answer: Equilibrium price is the price at which a product will naturally settle. If the price is set higher than the equilibrium price, there will be less demand, and a surplus of product will result. Producers will then lower the price to the equilibrium price to get rid of the surplus. If the price is set too low, there will be more demand, and a shortage of product will result. Then producers will raise the price to take advantage of the shortage.

44.

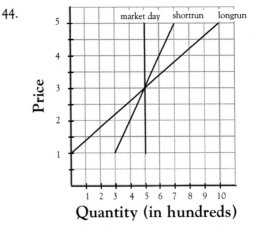

45. Students should draw a new demand curve parallel to the first and shifted to the right.

46. Students should draw a new demand curve parallel to the first and shifted to the right. A normal good is any good for which demand increases as income increases (and demand decreases as income decreases). An example of a good that is not a

normal good is an inferior good. Inferior goods are those for which demand decreases as income increases.

47. 1. Demand for zucchini will go down. 2. Demand for substitute goods will go up. 3. Answers will vary. Any green vegetable is reasonable.
4. complement (or related) good 5. Demand for mushrooms will go down.

48. A change in demand is any change that shifts the entire demand curve inward or outward on the graph. A change in quantity demanded is a reflection of a change in price and occurs along the demand curve. See the sample chart below.

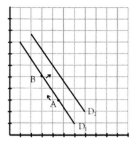

49.

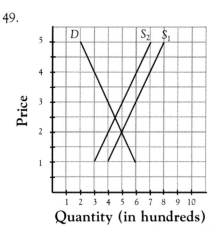

The new supply curve (S_2) raises the equilibrium price.

50. The supply curve will shift outward (to the right). An increase in supply will lower the equilibrium price.

51. 1. increases; 2. decreases; 3. decreases; 4. increases; 5. decreases; 6. increases

52. **Good = Jeans**

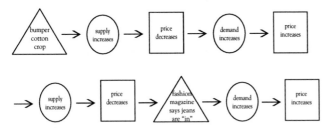

53. The equilibrium price is $5.

54. Answers may vary slightly.

1. The two products are perfect substitutes. An increase in price in one will likely lead to a proportional increase in demand for the other. 2. The two products are close substitutes. An increase in price for one may lead to a slight increase in demand for the other, although brand loyalty may exist that will keep this change from being significant. 3. The products are only sort of substitutes. Watching a movie in a movie theater is a different enough experience from watching it at home that an increase in ticket price may not have a significant effect, depending on the movie.

55. 1. All things being equal, neither brand can raise its price. Demand for the higher-priced brand will go down; consumers will simply buy the other brand. 2. Brand X could use marketing and advertising strategies to create brand loyalty, differentiating it as being better somehow (cooler, maybe) than Brand Y.

56. From left to right: 2, 3, 1; other answers will vary. Products chosen should be reasonable in terms of price elasticity of demand.

57. Answers will vary.

58. Answers may vary slightly. Sample answer: In the equation, Q stands for quantity along the demand curve. P stands for price along the demand curve. The subscripts 1 and 2 show that there are two different quantities and their related prices, and we are looking at how elastic demand is between

those two points on the curve. We need to average the two units, so we divide the two quantities, added together, by 2. Using the averages to find the percent change for P and Q, we arrive at a ratio of percent change in quantity over percent change in price.

59. A completely vertical line means that the same quantity is demanded at every price. Thus, the product is perfectly price inelastic. A completely horizontal line means that quantity is demanded at only one price. If the price is raised, no quantity will be demanded. Thus, the product is perfectly price elastic.

60. $P_e = 1.66$

61. Farmer Sutomi should increase the price of cheese, since demand is price inelastic. This means that people will still buy a quantity at the higher price that will increase revenues.

62. Answers may vary slightly, but should reach the following conclusion: Coffee would be inelastic in

demand due to the fact that it is habit-forming. People are unlikely to give it up immediately due to a price change. It may take people a while to accustom themselves to substitutes, but if the price remains high, people eventually will. The demand will become more elastic over the long run.

63. 1. b; 2. d; 3. a; 4. e; 5. c

64. An inferior good is a good for which an increase in income leads to a decrease in demand, since people will more likely choose close substitutes that are higher in cost. Examples will vary a good deal. Sample examples for food: ramen soup, boxed macaroni and cheese, canned vegetables, and so forth. For other products: two-door cars, less powerful computers, and so forth.

65. Product 2. Demand is price inelastic, meaning that consumers will still demand the product at the higher price once the tax is passed on. Therefore, revenues will be higher than for product 1, since fewer people would buy product 1 at a higher

price. The producer will also bear less of the burden with product 2.

66. Answers may vary slightly. Sample answer: Price is related to price elasticity of demand in that products that have a low price to start with tend to be less elastic in demand. For example, if the price of a candy bar goes up 10%, the change in price may not affect demand too much because the price represents a small amount compared with a person's overall income and expenditures. However, if housing prices go up 10%, the demand may be extremely elastic, since the cost of a home represents a large amount compared with a person's overall income and expenditures.

67. 1. a unit created by economists to measure an individual's increments of satisfaction from consuming goods and services; example: I receive 35 utils from riding my bicycle to the beach.
2. satisfaction from the consumption of goods and services; example: I receive utility from riding my bicycle to the beach. 3. the amount by which utility changes through consumption of one more unit of a good or a service; example: The first time I ride my bicycle to the beach in the summer, I receive 35 utils. When I ride to the beach again, my whole utility has gone up to 55, for a marginal utility of 20 utils. 4. total satisfaction received from the consumption of a good or a service; example: Two trips to the beach have given me a total utility of 55.

68. Answers will vary.

69. Marjorie receives 7 utils from her first box of peanut brittle, 5 from her second box, and 3 from her third box. Marginal utility decreases as one more unit of good is consumed, although total utility continues to increase.

70.

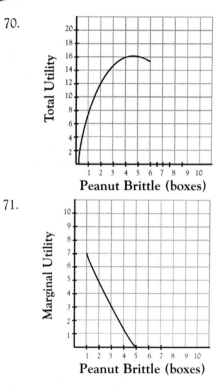

Peanut Brittle (boxes)

71.

Peanut Brittle (boxes)

72. Answers will vary. Students may answer that one more friend does not diminish marginal utility, or one more pet, or one more won game on the way to a state championship, and so forth.

73. Answers will vary.

74. 1. It will increase. If MU remains the same for the goods as price decreases, quantity demanded will increase, as more of a person's budget can be spent on the good. 2. They will decrease. The lower price of the good will cause more to be budgeted on it to maximize utility. A person will budget less for the other goods than before.

75. MU/P for any good creates an inverse relationship between marginal utility and price. There is an overall increase of marginal utility as price decreases. As price decreases, quantity demanded to fulfill utility increases; this is the same relationship as the demand curve.

76. Leo buys 4 CDs at equilibrium price $10. He was willing to buy one of these at $16 (+$6), an

additional CD at $14 (+4), and a third CD at $12 (+2), for a consumer surplus of $12.

77. Answers will vary. They should, however, cover the idea that a person making $25,000 a year may value a dollar more than a person who is a multimillionaire. A good example is a meal out at an expensive restaurant. For those of more limited means, this may be a rare occasion. It likely provides a tremendous amount of utility for a person of limited means compared with someone who can afford such a meal every day.

78. 1. a price set artificially low (lower than market equilibrium) through government intervention; example: rent control. 2. a price set artificially high (higher than market equilibrium) through government intervention; example: price of milk. 3. a type of price floor; a way of ensuring that farmers receive similar prices for their farm goods as they pay for nonfarm goods; example: price set for grain. 4. a guarantee to farmers of a certain price for a good set by the government— government subsidizes by buying the surplus; example: target prices set for agricultural goods

79. A price ceiling is a price artificially set below equilibrium price by a government. Price ceilings are set when demand is so high for the good in question that price is driven up beyond the means of most people. They are usually set for goods that people find necessary, such as a place to live. Society recognizes that for such goods, it is fair for people to have access to them.

80. When a price ceiling is instituted for a particular good, it shifts the supply curve for that good to the left. This means that producers will produce less of the good at the artificially set price. Supply of the good decreases. Government may need to intervene further to institute rationing to make sure there is fair access to the good.

81. Answers will vary. Students should cover the concept of fairness: The teacher provides a public

service in the community and should have access to housing there; the teacher's job is valuable to the community although it doesn't pay him or her enough to live in the city. Students should also cover the inefficiency that results from a price ceiling. The landlord has no incentive to maintain his or her buildings or bring new housing to market; this will just make supply even smaller. These are the main points; others may certainly be made.

82.

Quantity (in thousands)

At the price ceiling, 2,000 units will be produced.

83. Answers will vary. Points that should be covered: A black market may spring up; supply will decrease over time because producers don't want to supply at the artificial price; demand will then increase as supplies decrease; and so forth.

84. Price floors are prices set artificially high (above market equilibrium) by a government. They are usually set when an important industry (such as farming) becomes over-productive. Supply dramatically increases, and prices dramatically fall. Usually, they fall to such an extent that producers cannot continue to make a living.

85. When a price floor is instituted, the price is set above equilibrium, shifting the supply curve to the right. Producers are willing to supply more of the good at the artificially set price, but consumers are willing to buy less. This creates a surplus, which is usually bought up by the government.

86.

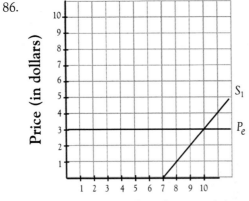

Quantity (in thousands)

At the price floor, 8,000 units will be produced.

87. 1. a firm owned by a single individual (or a family) who has sole legal responsibility; advantages: autonomy, lack of bureaucracy, local focus; disadvantages: unlimited liability. 2. a firm owned by two or more individuals who bear joint responsibility; advantages: more capital resources than in sole proprietorship, liability is shared; disadvantages: each person is liable for the others, necessity of consensus. 3. a firm set up as a separate legal unit; advantages: limited liability, ability to build capital through stock offerings; disadvantages: loss of autonomy, loss of local focus

88. Unlimited liability means that a sole proprietorship or partnership takes on all legal responsibility for the firm, including all of its debt. A proprietor's or partner's personal wealth can be appropriated to pay the debts of the firm. Limited liability means that a firm, having been incorporated, is its own legal identity. The owners/stockholders lose their investment if the firm goes bankrupt, but their other personal wealth is not subject to appropriation to pay the debts. Unlimited liability applies to proprietorships and partnerships. Limited liability applies to corporations.

89. sole proprietor; corporation; liability; charter; stock

90.   1. b; 2. a; 3. c. Stocks are ownership in a share of a company. Bonds are loans made to a corporation by individuals, paid back at interest.

91.   1. b; 2. c; 3. a; 4. d; 5. f; 6. e

92.   Answers will vary.

93.   Answers will vary. Sample answer: A fixed cost is one that is the same regardless of the quantity of good produced. For example, a fixed cost for an egg producer might be a chicken shed. Regardless of how many hens are in the shed, or how many eggs they produce, the cost for the shed is the same. A variable cost is one that goes up or down depending on quantity produced. For the egg producer, variable costs could be number of hens and the amount of chicken feed.

94.   For a given firm size, marginal return for added variable cost will get smaller and smaller as the fixed costs remain the same. Labor is the classic example, since there is a limit to how many people can work productively in a firm of a given size. But diminishing returns may apply to anything that constitutes a variable cost.

95.   Firm size dictates how much variable input (labor and so forth) can efficiently function to produce ideal output. Once firm size is too small for variable input, the firm becomes inefficient. The firm must invest fixed costs to create more capacity. This comes in the form of increasing plant size or investing in new technology.

96.   1. total cost; 2. total fixed cost; 3. total variable cost; 4. average total cost; 5. average fixed cost; 6. average variable cost; 7. marginal cost

97.   1. c; 2. a; 3. b; 4. d; 5. d

98.

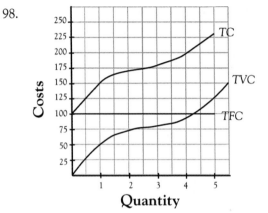

Q	TFC	TVC	TC
0	$100	$0	$100
1	$100	$50	$150
2	$100	$70	$170
3	$100	$80	$180
4	$100	$95	$195
5	$100	$130	$230

99. The completed table on the activity page is the same as the completed table for activity 98.

Q	AFC	AVC	ATC	MC
0	—	—	—	—
1	$100	$50	$150	$50
2	$50	$35	$85	$20
3	$33.30	$26.70	$6	$10
4	$25	$23.75	$48.75	$15
5	$20	$26	$46	$35

100. A fixed cost occurs regardless of quantity produced, and it remains the same over all quantities. So AFC is very high over small quantities and very low over high quantities. But it will never reach $0. Even at a fixed cost of $1 and a quantity of 1 million, there is an average cost incurred.

101. At first, AVC is high, before output reaches a point of efficiency. As more resources are put into

the firm (specialization of labor occurs and resources are put to their best use), AVC goes down. As the firm experiences diminishing returns, AVC creeps up again.

102. 1. explicit; 2. implicit; 3. explicit; 4. implicit; 5. implicit

103. 1. declining; 2. rising

104.

Q	ΔQ	TC	ATC	MC
0	0	$1,000	0	N/A
100	100	$1,150	$150	$1.50
200	100	$1,280	$130	$1.30
300	100	$1,395	$115	$1.15
400	100	$1,505	$110	$1.10
500	100	$1,610	$105	$1.05
600	100	$1,710	$100	$1.00
700	100	$1,825	$115	$1.15
800	100	$1,975	$150	$1.50
900	100	$2,185	$210	$2.10
1,000	100	$2,465	$280	$2.80

105. 1. b; 2. c; 3. a

106. A. MC = $1 and MR = $3; B. MC = $3 and MR = $3; C. MC = $6 and MR = $3. The firm should produce at point B.

107.

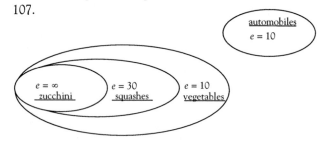

108. 1. A monopoly is a market structure with a single firm. No other firm is able to enter. 2. An oligopoly is a market structure with a small number of firms. It is extremely difficult for new firms to enter the market. 3. Monopolistic competition is a market structure with many firms. Firms can enter this market with some effort. 4. Perfect competition is a market structure with a

large number of firms. Entry into the market by another firm is easy.

109. An ideal market has completely homogeneous products (a given product is identical across consumers). It has perfect information for both buyers and sellers, in which consumers know everything about all products on the market, including where to find them at the lowest price. It has a large number of consumers and producers for every product. Finally, it does not have any barriers to entry for producers, such as control of a raw material by an existing firm.

110. When an oligopoly exists, firms end up pricing their goods based on the behavior of the other firms. When one firm lowers its price, the others lower theirs. Cartels are an outcome of this; rather then simply observing the behavior of others, firms simply get together and agree on a price. In this way, their behavior becomes monopolistic. An example of a cartel is OPEC.

111. Answers will vary somewhat. The classic example of a natural monopoly is AT&T. Once AT&T had the infrastructure in place (telephone poles, lines, and cable), it cost next to nothing to add on one more customer (after another, after another). No other firm could compete, since AT&T's marginal cost was so low.

112. There is a limit on how high prices can go before people stop buying the product in quantities that guarantee the highest return to the firm. If the quantity is such that $MR < MC$, the firm will lose revenue. However, since it is a characteristic of natural monopolies that MC is next to nothing, natural monopolies tend to have their prices regulated.

113. 1. It will shift toward the origin and become more price elastic. 2. They will go down. 3. Supply will increase, so price will decrease (*ceteris paribus*).

114. In perfect competition, there are a large number of firms in the market, and the products they offer

tend to be indistinguishable from everyone else's products. This leads to efficiency because some of the barriers to reaching equilibrium price (monopolistic behavior, differentiation of goods) are removed.

115. Answers will vary. The main arguments weigh the concerns of social benefit against the use of taxpayer money on an enterprise that cannot function in the market.

116. Answers will vary. All of these industries were bailed out because they provided some necessary good to the public.

117. Answers will vary. Sample answer: Wal-Mart is now the world's largest retailer. The company's huge size lets it buy products at deep discounts. This lets it undersell competitors, thus protecting and enlarging its market share.

118. The community's government can regulate the industry so that more people are willing (and able) to pay for phone service. The government could

set the price to increase demand. The firm would likely not want to produce at the set price, so the government would then likely provide a subsidy.

119. The firm will hire six people, the point at which MRP = MCL.

Laborers	MRP	MCL	MRP–MCL
0	—	—	
1	$30	$20	$10
2	$36	$20	$16
3	$40	$20	$20
4	$32	$20	$12
5	$28	$20	$8
6	$20	$20	$0
7	$16	$20	$–4
8	$10	$20	$–10

120. Answers will vary slightly. The argument against the minimum wage is that, if employers are forced to pay a wage higher than the market will bear,

they will simply "buy" less labor. Employers wish to keep marginal revenue and wages in balance.

121. Answers will vary. This is a complicated issue with many arguments for and against. As usual with economic policy, the two issues being weighed are equity (fairness) and efficiency.

122. In a monopsony, there is one employer in the market, and thus one "consumer" of labor. This allows the firm to set the price for labor, since there is generally an abundant supply of workers. A monopsony does not supply the usual market safeguards for labor (through competition among employers), so organized labor unions intervene to protect workers' rights.

123. Wealth constitutes the total assets of an individual, a family, or a firm. It is different from income in that income is a return on investment (of capital or labor) in the form of dividends, interest, or wages. Wealth is not necessarily just money, but investments, real estate, possessions,

and so forth. Income leads to wealth as it is saved; wealth leads to income as it brings return.

124. Answers will vary.

125. Answers will vary. The main disadvantage to calculating average income is that it does not take into account the cost of living, which is different in different areas of the country and the world. An advantage is that it is fairly easy to calculate and creates an accurate baseline. The disadvantage to the standard of living method is that what is considered an adequate standard of living changes over time and is different in different places. The bare standard of living in the United States and other developed countries may be unachievable elsewhere. Its advantage is that it reflects what people actually need in order to live rather than simply being an abstract number.

126. Answers will vary.

127. 1. f; 2. b; 3. a; 4. c; 5. d; 6. e

128. 1. A progressive tax is one in which the percent of

a person's income taken in tax increases as the person's income increases. The federal income tax is progressive. 2. A regressive tax is one in which the percent of a person's income taken in tax increases as the person's income decreases. Sales taxes on everyday goods (not luxury goods) are regressive. 3. A proportional tax is one in which the percent of a person's income taken in tax stays the same over all incomes. Several state income taxes are proportional.

129. A direct tax is any tax paid directly by the consumer to the government. Direct taxes include income taxes, property taxes, and most sales taxes. A hidden tax is a tax that is levied on the producer and passed along to the consumer in the cost of the good. Inventory taxes are often passed along this way (tax shift).

130. A tariff is a fee placed on an imported good. The tariff is often passed on to consumers in the form of an indirect tax, creating a tax shift.

131. A flat tax is a proportional tax. With this tax, everyone pays the same percentage of his or her income in income tax. The argument for a flat tax is that it is considered fair, plus it will stimulate the economy by leaving more money in the hands of high-earning consumers. The argument against it is that for low-wage earners, the percent taken from their wage may represent the difference between making ends meet and extreme hardship. In other words, 10% of $20,000 is $2,000, and 10% of $200,000 is $20,000, but the low-wage earner is left with even less of very little. A progressive income tax is a tax whose rate varies directly with the income of the person taxed. A progressive income tax seems less fair, but the argument for it is that high-wage earners can afford to pay a higher percentage of their income, taking the burden off of low-wage earners.

132. Answers will vary. Sample answer: The government believes that anyone who can afford a

luxury item such as a yacht can afford to pay a hefty tax on it without detriment. This is in contrast to a single mother trying to feed her children: She would feel the pinch of any amount of tax on necessities, even a small one. Opinions will vary greatly on the fairness of luxury taxes. Some students might feel that a person who has earned the money for a yacht has the right to buy one without an excessive tax (almost like paying a penalty for enjoying success). Others may point out that the tax will likely harm the yacht-building industry, the jewelry business, and so forth. Others may think that a tax structure such as this is fair, since each person is contributing based on his or her ability.

133. 1. Governments put a high tax on "sin" products in the hopes that people will stop using the products. In other words, they are trying to push the price higher on the demand curve. However, they also realize that sin products tend to be very price inelastic. This pretty much guarantees revenue from taxes on these products, since people will pay high prices for them. 2. Answers will vary. On one hand, people really should not smoke at all or drink too much, so as a deterrent, these taxes may seem fair. On the other hand, these taxes are very regressive, and they tend to hit those of low income hard. Should low-income people suffer more for their vices than high-income people?

134. 1. c; 2. e; 3. f; 4. a; 5. b; 6. d

135. 1. c; 2. e; 3. a; 4. d; 5. g; 6. b; 7. f

136. Answers will vary.

137. 1. The expenditure approach relies on counting up all final goods and services, including consumption by households, investment of equipment and other fixed goods by firms, consumption by government, and net exports by firms of goods to other countries. 2. The income approach relies on counting up all expenditures of

capital by firms for labor, interest earned, profit made by firms, rent for use of property, and proprietors' income.

138. Nominal GDP is measured in terms of current market prices. Real GDP is calculated by adjusting nominal GDP for price changes. This adjustment is made to give an accurate picture of economic growth.

139. 120

140. During a buildup for war or wartime itself, the federal government spends money on weaponry and defense, shifting the aggregate demand curve. Manufacturers respond by hiring workers, increasing the demand for capital goods and raw materials, and so forth.

141. The theory is, once people have more discretionary income (especially those who already tend to spend), aggregate demand will shift outward as more goods are demanded by consumers. This, then, stimulates production.

142. There will always be people who will only work for a higher wage. Paying people higher wages raises the cost of producing goods, causing the aggregate supply curve to slope upward and increasing the price level of goods.

143. Intermediate goods are those that go into making final goods. They are not included in the calculation of GDP because their price is reflected in the final cost for the good.

144. NDP is calculated by deducting capital depreciation from GDP. From there, indirect taxes (taxes placed on a good or a service) are subtracted to reach national income.

145. Answers will vary. Technology permits growth in ways that early economists would never have dreamed of. As computers get faster and smaller, for example, workers can get more done in less time, more information can be stored in smaller spaces, and so forth. Modern agriculture techniques have allowed farms to grow enormous

and to produce vast amounts. There are many other examples.

146. Answers will vary. Good examples are yard sales, babysitting, and barter between neighbors.

147. 1. c; 2. d; 3. a; 4. b

148. 1. d; 2. b; 3. c; 4. a

149. Autonomous consumption is consumption that people must do to survive. Examples are food, shelter, and so forth. This is a major concern in issues of wages, income, and poverty, since the costs of the necessities of life are often out of reach for some people. A major autonomous consumption issue that would be worthwhile to discuss with students is health care, which is already out of reach for many people on fixed incomes.

150. The Bureau of Labor Statistics defines unemployment as those people who are out of work and are actively looking for work. It does not include the underemployed, discouraged workers

(those who have given up looking), or homemakers. Other answers will vary.

151. This is easily one of the worst ways to save money; by the time the money leaves the mattress, it has lost its value every year at the rate of inflation.

152. 1. the trade of one good for another without the exchange of money; 2. paper money that is circulated without being backed by something of intrinsic value; 3. coins and bills; 4. the rate at which each dollar is exchanged per year

153. The barter system is a system of trade, in which one good is traded for another good without using money. With a small number of people, it can be advantageous: People don't have to work out a monetary value for their goods, but simply get something else that they want in exchange. With a larger number of people, barter becomes cumbersome. It is difficult to trade small things for large things; it is hard to determine exactly what people want and provide just that; carrying goods

from place to place becomes problematic. Other answers will vary.

154.   Answers will vary. Some terms students may write: barter, cash, credit card, debit card, check, traveler's check, and so forth.

155.   1. Money must be made out of something durable, since it would lose its value if it broke, rusted, corroded, and so forth. 2. People must be able to carry money easily from their homes to the market, or from market to market. 3. Money must be able to be broken down into small units. Otherwise, it would be difficult to exchange a large thing of value for something smaller and get "change" back. 4. Money must be made of homogeneous material that is divisible into identical units. Otherwise units would have different values. Money would not function properly if units were of varying value. 5. Money must be of a stable supply. If people could pick money out of the ground at will, the supply would not be stable and the money would be valueless. Money can't grow on trees!

156.   Gold is durable. It doesn't rust or tarnish. It is infinitely divisible and of completely homogeneous material, since it is an element. It is easily carried from one place to another. It is rare enough that the supply is relatively stable. Other nice features of gold are that it is malleable, so it can easily be made into coins, and it has decorative value.

157.   There is no difference. The U.S. government held gold and silver to back up the U.S. currency in circulation. This was the "gold standard" or "silver standard." The idea was that you could always cash in the currency for something of real value. But as long as the U.S. government continues sound monetary policy, fiat money (without gold or silver backup) works just as well.

158.   Denominations of U.S. currency now being produced: Coins—penny, nickel, dime, quarter,

half dollar, dollar: Bills—$1, $2, $5, $10, $50, $100. 1. Currency is made of paper, ink, copper, nickel, and zinc. 2. Answers will vary. Some may argue that this is not really money, since paper and base metals have no real value. Others may argue that, since government and citizens accept these items as money for innumerable transactions every day, it is money. Since this is an interesting discussion, explore the answers of the class.

159. 1. M1 money is the most liquid form of money; it includes currency, checking accounts, and traveler's checks. 2. M2 money includes M1 money, plus less liquid forms of money such as savings accounts, small-denomination CDs, and money market accounts. 3. M3 money includes M2 money, plus non-liquid forms of money such as large-denomination CDs and Eurodollars.

160. M stands for money, V stands for the velocity of money (the number of times it is exchanged), P stands for price, and Q stands for quantity. The equation is saying that there is an equal relationship between the amount of money in circulation times how often it changes hands and the prices of goods times their quantity.

161. Banks were established to hold people's money, provide loans, and, originally, to mint currency (chartered by the state). The federal government stepped in to control the money supply, establishing the First Bank of the United States, then the Second Bank, and, ultimately, the Federal Reserve. The Fed charters banks (some are still chartered by the states), controls the money supply, and provides a reserve for banks. The federal government also established FDIC, which protects depositors in the event of a bank failure.

162. Answers will vary. The banking system relies on the creation of "money" in the form of lending to represent its overall assets. It assumes that no day will occur when all depositors arrive at the bank to demand all of the money in their accounts.

Daily Warm-Ups: Economics

163. independent; Congress; twelve; must; 3%; equal
164. Paper currency is bills of all denominations, printed by the U.S. Bureau of Engraving and Printing. It isn't considered money until it is in circulation. Paper money is stored by the Fed until district banks ask for it, and it is put into circulation.
165. The banks use the Fed to clear checks. Kelly's bank sends the check to the regional Federal Reserve Bank, which clears the check; then it sends the check to Maine's regional Federal Reserve Bank, which sends the check to the issuer's bank, which debits the account.
166. 1. It decreases. 2. It shifts to the right. 3. It increases.
167. The Fed lowers the discount rate when it wants to encourage banks to lend money to people, typically during a recession. During an inflationary period, the Fed can raise the discount rate, discouraging bank lending.
168. Less unemployment tends to mean that, on the one hand, people are working at a higher wage rate and, on the other, that there is more demand overall for goods and services. These two features of low unemployment tend to raise prices.
169. 1. Do nothing. Aggregate supply and demand will reach equilibrium if left alone. 2. Use government intervention to shift the demand curve for labor (government programs). 3. Increase the aggregate supply by decreasing tax rates and decreasing government regulation.
170. A public good is one that does not decrease as people use it. A merit good is one that does decrease as people use it, and there are value judgments made on whom to provide it to. An example of a public good is a lighthouse. An example of a merit good is a public welfare program such as food stamps or Social Security.
171. Answers will vary, but should show an understanding of what constitutes a public good:

Multiple people can use it simultaneously, there can be any number of free riders, and one person's use does not diminish the good. The products listed vary as to how close they come to this ideal (the lighthouse and clean air being closer than a city park or education). Students should justify how a private firm could offer such a good (a fee for education, a toll to use the park). Those choosing the lighthouse or clean air may find it difficult to explain how a private company would be paid!

172. Answers will vary. Welfare, food stamps, and unemployment compensation are all examples of transfer payments.

173. The Social Security system was created in the 1930s as a way to ensure that older people had something to supplement their income after working age; it also pays survivor's benefits. The system works by having people who are presently working pay into the system; the money put into the system goes out to people as benefits. One of the issues currently being discussed about the Social Security system is the population of baby boomers who will soon be getting their benefits from it. It may be difficult for the current population of workers to put in enough money to cover that large population.

174. 1. international trade that is not subjected to tariffs and quotas; 2. goods and services bought in one country that are produced in other countries; 3. goods and services produced in one country that are sold in other countries; 4. an agreement between countries in which countries grant one another the same trading privileges; 5. global, international organization that deals with the rules of trade between nations; 6. organization of European nations whose goal is political and economic integration among its members; 7. free trade area made up of Canada, the United States, and Mexico

175. Answers will vary. The CEO will want to get the cheapest labor to be found; the student will likely want to boycott clothing manufactured in sweatshops; the low-income American will argue that clothing would not be affordable if it were made here.

176. NAFTA was controversial in large part because of concerns about low-wage labor in Mexico: Workers in the United States were concerned about industry and jobs going across the border, while others were concerned about exploitation of Mexican workers, firms avoiding U.S. pollution laws, and so forth.

177. Tariffs are placed on imports to make their prices similar to identical goods produced in the United States through a shifting of the tariff onto the consumer. This will cause the demand curve for the U.S.-produced good to shift less (that is, demand does not decrease as much) than it would if the import were offered at its lower price.

178. The EU is a free trade zone that allows the countries within to trade, for the most part, without an imposition of tariffs or quotas (although there are some exceptions on certain goods). There is also a benefit for some countries in going from their own currency to the euro.

179. LDCs are generally distinguished by their level of poverty, low economic growth rate, and high birth rate. Other features of LDCs are low life expectancy, high infant mortality rate, high illiteracy rates, and lack of infrastructure.

180. 1. A high population growth rate means a large percentage of the population is too young to work. The younger population also requires that more resources be put into the creation of consumer goods rather than capital goods. 2. The AIDS pandemic is disabling and killing off working adults, creating an even higher percentage of people younger than working age (not to mention creating a large population of orphaned children).